Praise for *The Transatlantic Gaze*

"...a meticulous work of love that juxtaposes some of the best Italian and American films produced since the end of World War II up until the second decade of the new millennium in order to unveil the influence of Italian cinema on American film ... The detailed analyses of this scrupulous work are of interest not only to scholars of cinema and Italian studies, but also to those engaged in comparative, cultural, American and Italian-American studies."

— *Journal of Modern Italian Studies*

"...an excellent reference for scholars ... Innovative, well-written and well-argued, *The Transatlantic Gaze* not only represents an important contribution to the field of film studies, but also to the area of Italian cultural studies, inserting itself into a series of works that study the influence of Italian culture but are written in English and thus directed towards an anglophone audience."

— *Journal of Italian Cinema and Media Studies*

"…insightful … In detailed readings and comparisons, and thanks in part to the well-chosen quotations that she meticulously analyzes, Carolan is masterful in acknowledging the tremendous impact that the Italian filmmakers have had on their American counterparts."

— *CHOICE*

"…Carolan has written an astutely focused text on a universally acknowledged subject, but one that is rarely covered these days, even in academia … this book is an excellent reference for scholars and could provide movie buffs or Italophiles with a wealth of film trivia."

— *San Francisco Book Review*

The Transatlantic Gaze

SUNY series in Italian/American Culture
_____
Fred L. Gardaphe, editor

The Transatlantic Gaze

Italian Cinema, American Film

MARY ANN McDONALD CAROLAN

SUNY
PRESS

Cover images: Cinecitta' publifoto / Olycom
                Hollywoodland sign courtesy of Photofest

Published by State University of New York Press, Albany

For information, contact State University of New York Press, Albany, NY
www.sunypress.edu

Production by Diane Ganeles
Marketing by Kate McDonnell

Library of Congress Cataloging-in-Publication Data

Carolan, Mary Ann McDonald.
  The transatlantic gaze : Italian cinema, American film / Mary Ann McDonald Carolan.
        pages cm. — (SUNY series in Italian/American culture)
  Includes bibliographical references.
  ISBN 978-1-4384-5025-4 (hc : alk. paper)—978-1-4384-5024-7 (pb : alk. paper)
  1. Motion pictures—United States—History—20th century.   2. Motion pictures—Italy—Influence.   I. Title.

  PN1993.5.U6C315 2013
  791.430973—dc23   2013014433

10 9 8 7 6 5 4 3 2 1

To Jim

Contents

List of Illustrations   ix

Acknowledgments   xiii

I.   Introduction   1

II.   Screen Idols and Female Admirers in *The White Sheik* (Fellini, 1952), *The Purple Rose of Cairo* (Allen, 1985), and *Nurse Betty* (LaBute, 2000)   15

III.   The Art Film Reconsidered: *Blow-Up* (Antonioni, 1966) and *Blow Out* (De Palma, 1981)   45

IV.   The Evolving Western: From America to Italy and Back in *Once Upon a Time in the West* (Leone, 1968) and *Kill Bill: Volumes 1 and 2* (Tarantino, 2003 and 2004)   61

V.   Neorealism Revisited by African American Directors in the New Millennium: *Precious: Based on the Novel "Push" by Sapphire* (Daniels, 2009) and *Miracle at St. Anna* (Lee, 2008)   85

VI.   Whither the Remake?   109

VII.   Conclusion   131

Notes   139

Bibliography   149

Index   163

Illustrations

1.1 *Quo vadis?* (Guazzoni, 1912) 7

1.2 *Ben-Hur* (Niblo, 1925) 9

2.1 Rudolph Valentino 19

2.2 Fernando Rivoli (Alberto Sordi) and Wanda
(Brunella Bovo) in *The White Sheik* 21

2.3 Shooting the *fotoromanzo* in *The White Sheik* 24

2.4 On the set behind the screen in *The Purple Rose of Cairo* 28

2.5 Cecilia (Mia Farrow) at the movies in *The Purple
Rose of Cairo* 29

2.6 Tom Baxter (Jeff Daniels) and Cecilia (Mia Farrow)
in *The Purple Rose of Cairo* 31

2.7 Betty (Renée Zellweger) working at the Tip Top in
Nurse Betty 34

2.8 Betty (Renée Zellweger) with cut-out of
Dr. David Ravell (Greg Kinnear) in *Nurse Betty* 35

3.1 Thomas (David Hemmings) photographs Veruschka
in *Blow-Up* 48

3.2 Thomas (David Hemmings) with his montage in
Blow-Up 52

3.3 Jack Terry (John Travolta) in the sound studio in
Blow Out 54

3.4 Jack Terry (John Travolta) makes his movie in
Blow Out 54

4.1 Initial duel in *Once Upon a Time in the West* between
Harmonica (Charles Bronson) and American guest stars 65

4.2 Harmonica (Charles Bronson) and Frank (Henry Fonda)
working out a deal in *Once Upon a Time in the West* 67

4.3 Jill (Claudia Cardinale) in *Once Upon a Time in
the West* 70

4.4 Beatrix Kiddo (Uma Thurman) makes her moves in
Kill Bill Vol. 1 79

5.1 Antonio (Lamberto Maggiorani) and Bruno
(Enzo Staiola) Ricci contemplate a brighter future in
Bicycle Thieves 86

5.2 Pina (Anna Magnani) tries to defend her man in
Rome Open City 87

5.3 Precious (Gabby Sidibe) in *Precious* 92

5.4 Precious (Gabby Sidibe) and Mary (Mo'Nique) at
home with Mongo (Quisha Powell) in *Precious* 98

5.5 Cesira (Sophia Loren) with Rosetta (Eleonora Brown)
in *Two Women* 99

5.6 Screen shot: Hole in ceiling in *Two Women* 100

5.7 Screen shot: Hole in ceiling in *Precious* 100

5.8 Spike Lee, wearing the Buffalo Solider insignia,
on the set of *Miracle at St. Anna* 105

6.1 Frank Slade (Al Pacino) and Charlie Simms
(Chris O'Donnell) in *Scent of a Woman* 111

6.2 Raffaella (Mariangelo Melato) and Gennarino
(Giancarlo Giannini) in *Swept Away* 113

6.3 Joanna (Goldie Hawn) and Dean (Kurt Russell) and
family in *Overboard* 115

6.4 Matteo Scuro (Marcello Mastroianni) and daughter
Tosca (Valeria Cavalli) at train station in
Stanno tutti bene 117

6.5   Frank (Robert De Niro) and Amy (Kate Beckinsale)
      in *Everybody's Fine*   118

6.6   Cabiria (Giulietta Masina) in *Nights of Cabiria*   119

6.7   Charity Hope Valentine (Shirley MacLaine) in
      Sweet Charity   119

6.8   Guido Anselmi (Marcello Mastroianni) conducts in *8½*   122

6.9   Guido Contini (Daniel Day-Lewis) and Stephanie
      (Kate Hudson) et al. in *Nine*   123

6.10 Nanni Moretti plays himself in *Dear Diary*   127

7.1   *Once Upon a Time in the West* poster   136

Acknowledgments

Little did I realize that participation in seminars organized by the Laboratorio internazionale della comuncazione in the Friuli region of Italy in the summers of 1983 and 1984 would lead me to write a book on cinema. Those seminars, under the direction of Professor Bruno DeMarchi of the Università Cattolica del Sacro Cuore of Milan, drew an international group of students from Eastern Europe (Poland and Yugoslavia mainly), Western Europe, and the Middle East. I was the lone American. I could not have realized then that this experience would be the beginning of thinking about Italian cinema as a transnational phenomenon. One summer we had the honor of discussing filmmaking with Cesare Zavattini, already well advanced in years but still keenly passionate about cinema as an art form. Our studies brought us together to share perspectives on neorealism and *commedia all'italiana*. I am grateful to have had this experience, which was supported by a grant through the Italian Cultural Institute in New York.

Serendipity brought me to Italy, but I ended up studying the language, literature, and culture of that country because of dedicated, demanding, and inspiring teachers. Professor Edward Bradley, known for his rigor, energy, and passion for all things Roman and Greek, led our Dartmouth Classics Foreign Study program in Rome in the fall of 1979. Edward was the consummate teacher and remains so to this day. Our friendship is the kind that sustains one in life, and for that I am eternally grateful. In graduate school at Yale, I studied with Paolo Valesio, who encouraged me to read widely and explore the nuances of modern Italian literature. Courses on Dante, Boccaccio, and Petrarch with Giuseppe Mazzotta led me eventually to write a dissertation with him on Manzoni. I learn from Giuseppe whenever we talk because of his truly encyclopedic knowledge of ideas that have shaped literature and culture from within and without the canon. The late María Rosa Menocal was a reader of my dissertation and a mentor who gave me great counsel on academic and professional matters. I wish I could share this book with her. At the end of my time in graduate school, Deanna Shemek arrived. She mentored me early in my career and instilled in me a disciplined approach to writing. Penny Marcus has been my interlocutor on this project as well as on others, and I appreciate her advice, nuanced understanding of Italian cinema and culture, as well as her insistence on clear writing. Watching and discussing movies with Penny and Allan is one of life's great pleasures. Conversations with John Freccero about *Blow-Up* have helped me appreciate how that film, like Dante's *Commedia*, offers myriad possibilities for analysis. Robert Farris Thompson, who was Master of Yale's Timothy Dwight College while I was a Resident Fellow, has taught me about the translation of culture from one continent to another through his passionate, sensitive, and disciplined study of African art. Thank you, Master T.

In the profession, I have had the opportunity to work with a number of colleagues whose experience and guidance have helped me enormously. Anthony Tamburri and Paolo Giordano, whom I met years ago at a conference, have organized lectures and symposia that have furthered the trajectory of Italian American studies. Their ideas have shaped the vanguard of Italian American studies, and their generosity and encouragement have nurtured a new generation of scholars in the field.

Early in my career at Fairfield, while preparing a course on the Italian American experience with a grant from the Humanities Institute of the College of Arts and Sciences at Fairfield University, I met author Anthony Riccio, whose books record the oral histories of Italian Americans. Our encounters in New Haven, both by chance and by design, always seem to inspire new ideas; his work in recording the stories of others is critical for our understanding of the immigrant experience. I have discussed this book, as well as other projects, with Peter Patrikis, whose keen editing and incisive thoughts always improve my work. I can always count on him to steer me in the right direction. James Peltz, Co-director of State University of New York Press, has provided encouragement and assistance from this manuscript's earliest days. I appreciate his professionalism and courtesy in all our interactions. I also wish to thank my production editor at the Press, Diane Ganeles, who did a superb job putting this book together.

I am thankful for the collegiality and dedication of my colleagues at Fairfield. I have benefited from discussions on film with Jiwei Xiao, who has taught me much about the nuances of her language and culture. Joel Goldfield has encouraged me, and I have learned from his dedication to and passion for teaching. My Italian colleagues past and present, Yael Eliasoph, Marilisa Beccalli, Vincent Morrissette, Michela Knight, Sara Diaz, Teresa Picarazzi, and Letizia Bellocchio, have made teaching at Fairfield a pleasure. Their collegial spirit and generosity is truly extraordinary. Philip Eliasoph welcomed me to the university years ago and continues to give sage advice. I have benefited from conversations about European film with Bob Webster, who also set a model for leadership in our department. Leo O'Connor's suggestions to watch certain films have led me inadvertently to materials used in this book, and convivial conversations over lunch have proved some of the most pleasant hours of my working life. Elizabeth Dreyer's clarity and humanity have inspired me for years. Louise Carcusa and Alexa Mullady are most professional, patient, and resourceful. They keep me sane, which is a tall order some days.

At Yale, Wesleyan, and Fairfield, I have had the pleasure of teaching students about Italian literature and culture, and about Italian cinema in particular. Their excellent questions have stimulated me to think creatively, and for that I am most grateful. It is a pleasure to follow the careers of those Fairfield students who have chosen to pursue graduate studies. I am grateful to Carol Chiodo in particular for the many hours she has spent discussing this project with me.

My friends have nurtured me both physically and psychically. Special thanks are due to Sue Kahil for encouraging me to write this book, and not another one that I thought I should write. Life at home would be much less interesting and much more somber if it were not for our fantastic neighbors Laura and Joe Elman and Maria and Dexter Peavy. We are indeed fortunate to have landed where we did, especially when the weather turns nasty. So many meals, conversations, and celebrations with Susan and Paul Fiedler and their children Lizzy, Jacob, and Matt have sustained me throughout the writing of this manuscript. Encouragement and food make a delicious combination, so thank you. Other friends, who seem to have been with me for life, Emily and Eduardo Anhalt, Debbie and Steve

Berger, Bill and Julia Weaver Bernstein, Joann and Walter Kloss, Alice Galuszka Papsun, Joyce and Paul Perrella, and Kelli Hallock Simmons, have always believed in my ability to finish this book, even when I may not have. Kristin, Ric, Claire and Matthew Court, although no longer on the East Coast, remain close in my heart.

Our dear friends in Italy, Piera Angeletti and Mauro Caracuzzo, their children, Bianca and Viola, and Angela and the late Adamo Angeletti always extend a hearty welcome and make me feel completely at home in Rome. I met Anna and Roberto Rovelli my first year in graduate school; they remain close friends and wonderful interlocutors. They taught me how to drive in Palermo, which is no mean feat. Speaking of driving, I must thank Peggy Stewart for agreeing to go to Italy so many years ago; if it had not been for my fearless copilot, I might never have returned.

Fairfield University has granted me sabbatical leave to work on various chapters of this book over the years. An initial grant from the Humanities Institute at the university allowed me to prepare my seminar on the Italian American experience, a course that led me to the premise of this book, namely the distinct contributions that Italy has made to political, social, and artistic life in the United States. I am thankful for the sustained support of this project by Dean Robbin Crabtree. Additionally, the university, through the office of the Dean of the College of Arts and Sciences, has provided funding for the illustrations in this book. These illustrations, with the exception of the cover image of Cinecittà (from PUBLIFOTO/OLYCOM), appear courtesy of Photofest.

Portions of two chapters appeared previously in print: "Antonioni's Doubting Thomas: Resurrection and Self-Discovery in *Blow-Up*," *Romance Languages Annual* 12 (2003): 203–208; and "Leone's Lone Lady: A New Perspective of Women in *Once Upon a Time in the West*," *Romance Languages Annual* 11 (1999): 261–268.

This book would not have been possible if it were not for the love and affection of my family. Through marriage, my family has grown to include Stephen Carolan, Mark Carolan, Cathy Carolan and Greg Cohelan, Katie Cohelan, Celia and Jon Nelson, Jameson and Sarah Nelson, as well as James Carolan and his late wife, Eileen. Time with them is marked by intelligent conversation and much laughter. My brothers, Michael and John McDonald, unwittingly steered me to genres that I may not have chosen myself during long afternoons of watching war films and Westerns in addition to every imaginable type of sporting competition. I am grateful for that, as well as for the comfort and companionship, both at home and away, of the rest of the McDonald clan: Deirdre, Erin, Brittany, and Lindsey and Stephanie, Sam, and Ellison. I have never doubted the unconditional love of my parents, Frank and Mary McDonald. Theirs is one of the greatest gifts of all. I only hope that I can bestow the same gift on my own children. Maria and Anna have helped me become a better person, a better teacher, and a better scholar through their incisive questions, brilliant insights, and good humor. Their impressions and ideas have shaped mine, and for that I am appreciative. My husband, Jim, whom I met in graduate school decades ago, has always believed in me. After all these years, he still makes me laugh. I dedicate this book to him.

January 2013
Woodbridge, Connecticut

I

Introduction

"Sono da sempre un grande appassionato di cinema italiano: per questa ragione quando è capitata quest'occasione di realizzare Gangs of New York a Cinecittà mi sono sentito emozionato anche all'idea. Prima di tutto perchè è il simbolo del cinema italiano. E poi perchè qui ci sono artigiani assolutamente straordinari."

("I have always been a fan of Italian cinema. For that reason, when the opportunity arose to shoot *Gangs of New York* at Cinecittà, I jumped at the chance. First of all because it represents Italian cinema, and also because it has the most extraordinary artisans.")[1]

—Martin Scorsese

"Cinecittà è per me come gli studios che più conosco, perchè come a Hollywood è un luogo dove si può fare qualsiasi cosa, e farla bene."

("Cinecittà is like all the studios that I know best, because it, like Hollywood, is a place where you can do anything, and do it well.")

—Francis Ford Coppola

The above quotes from Martin Scorsese and Francis Ford Coppola greeted visitors to the Palazzina Fellini in 2012 as part of the exhibition *Cinecittà Si Mostra/Cinecittà Shows Off* that celebrated the Italian studios' place in the history of world cinematography. Their comments illustrate the premise of this book, namely the profound impact that Italian cinema has had on filmmaking in the United States. In the past, examinations of international cinematic exchange have focused primarily on the ways in which the American film industry has exerted its predominance worldwide. The notable cultural hegemony of the United States in cinema has produced English titles such as *Exporting Entertainment: America in the World Film Market* (Thompson, 1985), *Hollywood in Europe: Experiences of a Cultural Hegemony* (Ellwood and Kroes, 1994), *'Film Europe' and 'Film America': Cinema, Commerce and Cultural Exchange 1920–1939* (Higson and Maltby, 1999), *Global Hollywood* (Miller et al., issue 1, 2001 and issue 2, 2004), *World Cinema's 'Dialogues' with Hollywood* (Cooke, 2007), *Hollywood and Europe: Economics, Culture, National Identity, 1945–1995* (Nowell-Smith and Ricci, 2007), and *Post-War Italian Cinema: American Intervention, Vatican Interests* (Treveri Gennari, 2009). Scholarship in English on the relationship between the two film cultures has focused primarily on the representation of Italians in American film. In *Re-viewing Italian Americana* (2011), Tamburri ("Italian Americans and the Media: Cinema, Video, Television" 13–59) chronicles the representation of Italians on-screen in the United States. Bertellini, in *Italy in Early American Cinema: Race, Landscape, and the Picturesque* (2009), has focused in particular on the representations of Italians in the early days of cinema as well as on film viewing in Italian emigrant communities. Bondanella offers a historical critique of five character types from the early days to the present in *Hollywood Italians: Dagos, Palookas, Romeos, Wise Guys and Sopranos* (2004). Cavallero's *Hollywood's Italian American Filmmakers: Capra, Scorsese, Savoca, Coppola, and Tarantino* (2011) represents a new direction in scholarship insofar as it examines the Italian Americans behind the camera rather than those in front of it. In Italy, critics such as Di Biagi in *Italoamericani tra Hollywood e Cinecittà/ Italian Americans between Hollywood and Cinecittà* (2010) have also focused on the representation of Italians on-screen in the United States. Muscio, in *Piccole Italie, grandi schermi: scambi cinematografici tra Italia e Stati Uniti, 1895–1945/Little Italies, Big Screens: Cinematic Exchanges between Italy and the United States, 1895–1945* (2004), analyzes the presence of Italians and Italian Americans in American films in the larger context of cultural exchange between Italy and the United States before the end of the Second World War. In *Hollywood Italian: gli italiani nell'America di celluloide/Hollywood Italian: The Italians in American Film* (1998), Casella relates the experiences of Italian and Italian American directors, writers, actors, and producers in Hollywood while considering the prejudices and expectations encountered by this particular ethnic group. Bizio and Laffranchi, in *Gli italiani di Hollywood: il cinema italiano agli Academy Awards/Hollywood Italians: Italian Cinema at the Academy Awards* (2002), examine Hollywood's estimation of award-winning performances by Italian talent. By way of introduction to that text, Bizio (9–24) clearly acknowledges the Italian impact on Hollywood.

The Transatlantic Gaze highlights specific instances of dialogue between Italian and American directors in a series of close readings of Italian and American films of various genres to investigate how filmmaking techniques and narratives have been translated across the Atlantic. Italian masters such as Vittorio De Sica, Federico Fellini, Sergio Leone, and Michelangelo Antonioni have imprinted their techniques and sensibilities on American directors such as Spike Lee, Lee Daniels, Woody Allen, Neil LaBute, Quentin Tarantino, Brian De Palma, and others. Focusing primarily on the period following World War II to the first decade of the twenty-first century, this investigation seeks to contextualize Italian and American film criticism in a transatlantic framework that surrounds and informs cinematic production in the two countries. The essays in this book examine the profound connections between these film cultures that have resulted in an ongoing conversation between particular directors across the Atlantic. They also point to genre as an interpretative key to understanding the underlying premises of this cultural exchange.

This book acknowledges the long-standing history of exchange in terms of cinematic technology and content between the United States and Europe. In the late nineteenth century, inventors from both sides of the Atlantic, including Thomas Edison in the United States and the Lumière brothers in France, worked to develop a technology that would set in motion previously static photographic images. The new phenomenon of the moving picture captivated early audiences with short scenes, lasting only several minutes each, of everyday life depicting workers leaving a factory, a man watering his garden, and a baby eating dinner with his parents. From its origins, cinema offered a form of entertainment that appealed globally. Because of their easy adaptability to diverse cultures, silent films moved swiftly and seamlessly from one country to another with translated inter-titles.

Collaboration and competition across the Atlantic characterized the relationship between Italian and American film industries.

At times a tug-of-war for artistic and financial prominence, the relationship between the film industries in Italy and America focused on Hollywood and the centers of Italian film production, initially Torino (or *Filmopoli*, as journalists called that city) and later Cinecittà. The American filmmakers admired and sought to imitate the successes produced by the first Italian cinematic golden age, which lasted from approximately 1909 to 1916. Martin Scorsese, in his introduction to the screening of the remastered copy of *Cabiria* (Pastrone, 1914) at Cannes in 2006, said that watching that film disabused him of certain falsehoods regarding the history of cinema, including the belief that American directors such as D. W. Griffith and Cecil B. DeMille were responsible for introducing the lengthy historical epic, the use of the dolly, and diffuse light (9). These important realizations came relatively late to Scorsese, whose 1999 documentary *My Voyage to Italy* is a poignant acknowledgment of the director's indebtedness to Italian cinematography from neorealism to Fellini.

Cabiria, an epic tale of the capture, enslavement, and eventual release of the daughter of a wealthy Roman family during the second Punic War, quickly became an international phenomenon after its release in Italy in 1914. This saga of Rome and Carthage delighted audiences in Europe, including Hungary and Russia, as well as those in South America, India, Egypt, Japan, and Australia (Caranti 167). The diffuse distribution of *Cabiria*, deemed "kolossal" because of its budget as well as its wide-ranging plot, resulted in the projection of Pastrone's film in all major American cities as well as in more rural parts of the United States including West Virginia and Arkansas. The film's international reach appears in a fictional context as well: in Mike Newell's *Love in the Time of Cholera* (2007), the lovers Florentino Ariza and Fermina Daza meet again after many years at the screening of Pastrone's masterpiece in Cartagena, Colombia. This meta-cinematic moment in the filmic interpretation of Gabriel García Márquez's lyrical novel locates the narrative in a historical context while marking the time two star-crossed lovers have spent apart. *Cabiria*'s presence within another film further underscores the fact that the release of Pastrone's film was a worldwide sensation.[2]

D. W. Griffith's encounter with *Cabiria* demonstrates the dynamic relationship between Italian and American film in the early years of cinema. The American director traveled from Los Angeles to San Francisco to see the Italian masterpiece and to view the effects of Pastrone's inventive use of the dolly (*carrello* in Italian), which allowed him to mediate the lengths of his shots. After viewing this three-hour epic, Griffith announced his decision to realize a work that he had long envisioned, the film that would become *Intolerance* (1916).[3] Pastrone's techniques and expertise at rendering battle scenes, naval adventures, volcanic eruptions, and religious sacrifices on two continents inspired Griffith to tackle the enormous feat of interweaving tales of intolerance from four different time periods. *Intolerance* frames a contemporary love story of a young woman and man who are separated by the powerful forces of "good" in the Temperance movement against three distinct historical instances of intolerance—the life and persecution of Christ, the plight of the Huguenots in France, and religious rivalry in Babylonia. The Babylonian segment, with its ornate depiction of the ancient city, complete with towering sculpted elephants, pays particular homage to *Cabiria's* epic representation of southern Italy and Carthage. Griffith undoubtedly felt personally challenged by the magnificence of Italian film artistry when news regarding the filming of his *Judith of Bethulia* (1913) was overshadowed by the release of Guazzoni's masterpiece *Quo vadis?* in 1912. Wyke (7) emphasizes the competitive nature of this relationship when she states, "It took D. W. Griffith to outdo the Italians in terms of spectacle. With his production of *Intolerance* in 1916, Griffith set a standard for screen spectacle that has seldom been equaled." Jarratt (19) agrees with Wyke's assessment that exemplary Italian films such as *Cabiria* spurred the American director to produce his best work.

Pastrone's *Cabiria* demonstrates the genius of Italian silent cinema. In the 1910s, Italian films were recognized for their ability to render historical epics in a realistic yet monumental fashion. Early Italian cinema benefited from the country's abundant Mediterranean light and myriad monuments from classical antiquity as well as from the willingness of thousands of Italians to serve as extras for very low wages. These resources allowed Italian directors to produce elaborate pictures that incorporated spectacular settings, huge crowds, and advanced special effects. The artistic mastery of Italian directors, costume and set designers, and technicians also contributed significantly to cinematic excellence. By 1911, three firms, Itala-film and Società Anonima Ambrosio in Turin and Cines in Rome, shot 60 percent of Italian films, including the only four movies lasting more than an hour. In that year, Itala-film shot one film every three days, Ambrosio one every two days, and Cines one film per day (Sorlin 30). Most were short films, of five to ten minutes in duration, that were shown in dance halls and theaters. They were remakes of previous movies, imitations of foreign productions, documentaries, or one-man shows. The target audience was primarily domestic, not international. Production increased dramatically throughout the decade, from 16 feature-length films in 1912 to 252 in 1916 (Sorlin 31). This increase was due to a number of factors, but agreements with foreign distributors played a particularly important role.

The new medium of cinema provided a vehicle to reconstruct history with a precision that surpassed previous forms of representation such as the novel, historical fiction, or documentary sources, according to Wyke (9). Historical epics also mitigated against the disdain some expressed for the new art form of cinematography. After viewing the audience's overwhelmingly positive response to Pastrone's work, a critic concluded in the Naples journal *Film* on April 23, 1914, "*Cabiria* is something that will last. It will last because at that instant the vulgar art of cinema ceases and history succeeds, true history" (qtd. in Wyke 9).

Guazzoni's film *Quo vadis?* (1912), which is recognized as the first feature-length film, changed the course of American cinema when it premiered in New York in 1913. Based on a novel by Polish Nobel laureate Henryk Sienkiewicz, the film recounts the great love affair between two slaves, one Roman, the other Christian, during Nero's savage reign. George Kleine, a founder of Kalem Company with Samuel Long and Frank J. Marion, saw the spectacular production in Europe and returned to the United States determined to present the film despite its length. He bought the American rights to the film and presented it to the manufacturers and officials of the Patents Company and General Film Company and a number of prominent exhibitors. They were skeptical that American audiences would be able to sit through the entire nine reels. Yet Kleine was undeterred. He rented the Astor Theater on Broadway, advertised *Quo vadis?* as a form of entertainment similar to a stage play, and charged an unusually high admission of $1.00. The day after the film's opening on April 21, 1913, the *New York Times* praised the film, which lasted more than two hours, as "the most ambitious photo drama that has yet been seen here." Citing the gladiatorial arena in particular as "almost painful, so faithfully do they paint a picture of ruthless cruelty," the review went on to compliment the photography, lighting, and acting, as well as the direction of "the small army of supernumeraries" in *Quo vadis?* A road show with twenty-two stops throughout the United States and Canada followed the film's triumphant New York debut. Perhaps most importantly, *Quo vadis?*'s resounding commercial success illustrated that the American public was willing to pay for artistic films, long appreciated in Europe but previously unavailable in the United States under the conditions of General Film Company Trust, established in 1909 by Edison, Biograph, and others (Hampton 106–107).[4]

World War I dealt a significant blow to the artistic and financial success of Italian films. European cinema had felt the impact of American cultural hegemony as early as 1912, but the war interrupted Continental attempts to strike back at the rise of American film, according to Hampton (351). Brunetta offers a number of causes, in addition to the American "invasion" of the European film industry, for the decline of Italian cinema in the 1920s. He cites economic recession,

Figure 1.1. *Quo vadis?* (Guazzoni, 1912).

disorganization, excessive taxes, and increased costs among other factors (*Cent'anni* 132–136). In the United States, the development of film studios, first on the East Coast, then in California, led to the rise of American domination in film. These studios sought to capitalize on the economy of scale that allowed them to create, produce, and distribute films in an efficient manner. Whereas in the 1910s the creativity and inventiveness of Italian directors influenced filmmaking in the United States, in the 1920s American films flooded the Italian market and remained the primary entertainment for Italian audiences throughout the fascist period. With its infrastructure severely diminished by World War I, the Italian film industry suffered a significant decline in the 1920s. The number of indigenous films decreased from 220 in 1920 to fewer than 12 in 1927–1928 (Bondanella *Italian Cinema* 12). Foreign films, and American films in particular, satisfied strong Italian demand for the medium. Italy was not alone in this phenomenon, because more than 90 percent of the pictures shown in most foreign countries were American. These films wielded broad commercial influence, for wherever American films penetrated, trade established a firmer foothold (Hampton 353). Revenues from foreign sales of American pictures represented 25 to 40 percent of their total earnings in the period between 1926 and 1928 (Hampton 357).

The 1920s also witnessed the arrival in Italy of American productions. Unscathed by the experience of World War I, the film industry in the United States exploited Italy for its wealth of talent and natural beauty. Leading directors such as Henry King and George Fitzmaurice worked in Italy with popular actors of the day such as Lillian Gish, Ronald Colman, Barbara LaMarr, and Lionel Barrymore on films such as *The White Sister* (1923), *Romola* (1924), and *The Eternal City* (1923), according to Soares (75). *Ben-hur* (Niblo, 1925), the most celebrated American production in Italy of the time, also contributed significantly to the decline of the Italian film industry as it diverted Italian artistic and technical talent from domestic production (Bondanella *Italian Cinema,* 12). This epic tale of two childhood friends, the Israelite Judah Ben-hur and the Roman officer Messala, who meet again after many years when Judah's misstep causes Messala to punish him harshly, was an international phenomenon. Judah, now a galley slave on a Roman ship, impresses the Roman general with his strength and loyalty and ultimately wins his freedom. Upon his triumphant return home as a celebrated athlete, Ben-hur can focus only on avenging Messala's earlier treatment of him. When Mussolini promised Louis B. Mayer, the producer of *Ben-hur,* assistance in finding facilities, he did not realize that this production would deal a devastating blow to the already crippled Italian film industry (Bondanella *Italian Cinema* 11–12).

The Italian production of *Ben-hur* was a spectacle in itself, as evidenced by the stories that circulated in the international press. *Photoplay* closely reported Hollywood's response to the missteps of the calamitous production in March 1925. The film magazine told of labor disputes and strikes organized by the socialists, who tried to bring down the fascist government; chaotic working conditions in Rome's Cines studio; technical problems with staging sea battles; poor morale among the American cast; and steep increases in the costs of film production. Critical changes, including the director (Fred Niblo replaced Charles Brabin) and lead (Ramon Novarro replaced George Walsh in the title role of Judah Ben-hur), caused further delays. The studio's first choice for this important role, the divo Rudolph Valentino, was

Figure 1.2. *Ben-Hur* (Niblo, 1925).

unavailable because of his involvement in a lawsuit with the studios (Leider 237). An article in *Photoplay* aptly described the travails of this production: "If a bad beginning makes a good ending, *Ben-hur* will be the greatest picture of all time" (Soares 81). The cost of the film's production ballooned; by mid-1924, outlays had skyrocketed from a projected $1.25 million to close to $2 million. Niblo and MGM executives blamed the excessive production costs on the Italian workers, but others pointed to mismanagement of the film's production as the reason for the delays and cost overruns. Several days after arriving in Rome to replace Brabin as director of the film, Niblo wired Louis B. Mayer in Hollywood that they would have to start from scratch: "Condition serious. Must rush work before November rains; no sets or lights available before August 1st. 200 Reels of film wasted; bad photography; terrible action" (Soares 83). Arid, hot weather caused additional problems with filming the chariot races and desert scenes. A famously disastrous scene at sea worsened the situation and ultimately resulted in the production's return to Hollywood. In rough seas off the coast of Livorno, 150 miles north of Rome, one of the Roman galley replicas caught fire, causing many extras, who had been paid additional sums for hazardous work, to panic and jump overboard fully clad in heavy armor. Several could not swim, even though all extras had declared their ability to do so. Reports of lives lost during production varied from one to three (Soares 85). Prior to the naval battle, the galleys had been deemed unseaworthy, and therefore the attack of the pirate ships on the Roman boat (where Ben-hur's valiant rowing impressed the commander whose life he would ultimately save) had to be staged at anchor.

American cinema dominated the Italian market during the *ventennio* (twenty years) of fascist rule. The government encouraged film viewing by regulating the cost of attendance. As Sorlin (74) points out, the price of a movie ticket remained constant at 2.00 Lire during the five-year period between 1932 and 1937, while the cost of pasta rose from 2.52 lire per kilogram to 3.20 lire per kilogram during the same time period. Evidently, entertainment was critical for the regime; its relationship to the country's defense was readily apparent in the inaugural ceremony for Cinecittà in 1937, which depicted Mussolini as a cinematographer against the banner exclaiming "*Il cinematografo è l'arma più forte*" ("Cinema is the strongest weapon"). Film was used for propagandistic ends as evidenced by the mandatory screening of short LUCE (*L'unione cinematografica educativa*) documentaries before feature films that depicted fascist agricultural policies (and the draining of marshlands in particular) directed at improving rural life, traditional folklore, and the celebration of work done in the countryside. Mussolini's life, deeds, and travels were also frequently portrayed in these short works (Sorlin 51–52).

In the 1930s, Italians realized that they had a lot to learn from the Americans about film production. To that end, in October 1937, Benito Mussolini's son Vittorio, the editor of *Cinema,* visited Hollywood along with the cultural minister, Luigi Freddi. Their visit was made partly to solidify RAM (Roach and Mussolini), a proposed $5 million joint venture between the two countries to produce "cinemaoperas" such as *Rigoletto, Aida, Tosca,* and *La Traviata.*[5] This joint company, which was supposed to make documentary newsreels promoting Italy as well, eventually failed.

Mussolini was cognizant of the importance of propaganda for his regime, which resulted in the establishment of LUCE in the 1920s to produce newsreels and documentary films, followed by the foundation of the Venice Film Festival (1932) and the *Centro Sperimentale di Cinematografia* (1935), then and now the premier Italian film school, and the creation of the studios at Cinecittà (1937), as well as the dedication of funds and awards for the encouragement and support of indigenous film production through taxes on imported films (Sorlin 70). Yet in 1938, the year after Vittorio Mussolini visited Hollywood, his father granted ENIC (*Ente nazionale industrie cinematografiche*) a monopoly in the film industry, causing MGM, Paramount, 20th Century Fox, and Warner Brothers to withdraw from the Italian market. It would take ten years for the collaboration between the two national film industries to resume.[6]

The postwar period witnessed the return of American film production and distribution to the European continent. In 1948 Mervyn LeRoy began filming a remake of Guazzoni's *Quo vadis?,* which had been an international success following its release in 1912. This film, which premiered in 1951, represented a significant milestone for relations between the cinemas of Italy and the United States. In his autobiograpy, LeRoy (171) tells of the willingness and ability of Romans to serve as extras in the late 1940s: "The Italians, I found, were born actors. They loved being in front of a camera, even if they were with 59,999 others, and each one of them felt it was his picture." The crowd scenes in *Quo vadis?* served both as a hiding place for the established actress Elizabeth Taylor (who sought a break from her then husband, Nicky Hilton), and as the place of discovery for the young, unknown beauty, Sophia Loren, who later thanked the director for launching her career. LeRoy (172–173) recounts in great detail the difficulties trainers had coaxing the lions to be aggressive because of the Roman heat during late-afternoon shoots and the inventive strategies he used to film the animals devouring Christians in the arena.

Cinema benefited from the *miracolo economico* (economic miracle) that swept Italy in the 1950s.[7] Later in that decade, American directors returned to Rome to film yet another version of *Ben-hur* (1959), directed by William Wyler and starring Charlton Heston in the title role. Rome became the destination for directors, actors, and the international jet set. In the 1950s and 1960s, the Via Veneto attracted talent from around the world, and Cinecittà was called "Hollywood on the Tiber." The cover story in *Time* on August 16, 1954 reported the astounding pace of the Italian film industry's revival: from 1948 to 1953, production increased from 54 to 145 films, revenues grew from $8.8 million to $48 million, and 3,278 new theaters opened in Italy. During the same time, 5,000 theaters closed in the United States. Despite the ravages of World War II, including Cinecittà's use as a refugee camp,[8] the Italian film industry was now second only to Hollywood. Fellini's portrayal of the internationally recognized celebrities and socialites who frequented Roman clubs and discotheques in *La dolce vita* (1960) captured this phenomenon for American viewers. In Rome in the 1960s, Joseph L. Mankiewicz filmed *Cleopatra* (1963), which gained notoriety as one of the most expensive films ever made. Starring Elizabeth Taylor and Richard Burton, the film cost an estimated $25 to $40 million (instead of the $2 million that had been budgeted) and lasted an astonishingly long 192 minutes (320 minutes for the director's cut).

The transatlantic exchange of ideas and themes between Italian and American film has continued from the 1960s until the present day. In the past fifty years, there have been far fewer milestones that mark critical intersections in the relationship between these two cinemas. But as American cinema became ascendant in Italy as well as elsewhere in mass culture, the influence of Italian directors and themes remained pervasive, although largely unacknowledged. The future of Italian cinema seemed particularly bleak in the 1980s, when Cinecittà suffered major financial woes and no alternative studios emerged before it was privatized by the Italian government in 1998. The Italian government has retained the title to the land while private entities conduct business there. More recently, another controversy engulfed the studios: in the summer of 2012, artisans at Cinecittà struck for three months to protest the proposed building of a luxury hotel and theme park as part of a revitalization plan at the studios. The matter was resolved through negotiations with unions in time for shooting to begin in mid-October 2012 on Paul Haggis's romantic drama *Third Person*, starring Casey Affleck, Liam Neeson, Mila Kunis, and Olivia Wilde. The studios will add state-of-the-art facilities in an attempt to keep them viable (Vivarelli). Despite these travails, in the late twentieth century and early part of the twenty-first century, American directors such as Francis Ford Coppola (*The Godfather Part III*, 1990), Martin Scorsese (*Gangs of New York*, 2002), and Wes Anderson (*The Life Aquatic with Steve Zissou*, 2004) have filmed works at Cinecittà. The Italian studios will survive, perhaps because of what Nochimson refers to in painterly terms as the "pentimento effect." When one visits Cinecittà, according to her, past productions appear to seep through the sets and locales, just as the past bleeds into present-day life in the city of Rome.

The essays in this volume document the sustained and profound artistic impact of Italian cinema on filmmakers in the United States, with particular emphasis on the genres of comedy, art film, Western, and neorealism. We begin by examining recurrent themes from Fellini's *Lo sceicco bianco/The White Sheik* in Woody Allen's 1985 film *The Purple Rose of Cairo* (as well as in *To Rome with Love* in 2012) and in Neil LaBute's *Nurse Betty* (2000). This essay focuses as well on the iconic Latin lover and Italian emigrant Rudolph Valentino and includes a reading of the *fotoromanzo* (photoplay), a popular literary form that combined elements of the comic book with photography, as key to understanding the powerful effect of cinema on the female psyche. A consideration of Michelangelo Antonioni's art film *Blow-Up* (1966), which resonated with directors and viewers throughout the world, follows. Fifteen years after that film's release, Brian De Palma wrote and directed *Blow Out* (1981), a decidedly political take on Antonioni's meditation on the merits and limits of the art of photography. The investigation continues with an analysis of Sergio Leone's role in the evolution of the Western. Leone, along with Sergio Corbucci and others, invented the so-called spaghetti Western.

This derisive term, coined by critics in the United States, refers to the Italian interpretation of the quintessential American genre. Elements and ideas employed by Leone, such as excessive violence and a new interpretation of a woman's role, had a direct impact on the American director Quentin Tarantino. His *Kill Bill* saga (2003, 2004) plays off elements of Leone's *C'era una volta il West/Once Upon a Time in the West* (1968). The next essay investigates the reappropriation of neorealist stylistics and motifs in the works of contemporary African American directors Lee Daniels (*Precious*, 2009) and Spike Lee (*Miracle of St. Anna*, 2008). We conclude by evaluating the growing phenomenon of the American remake of popular Italian films. Recent examples of this trend include *L'ultimo bacio* (Muccino, 2001)/ *The Last Kiss* (Goldwyn, 2006), *Stanno tutti bene* (Tornatore, 1990)/ *Everybody's Fine* (Jones, 2009), and *8½* (Fellini, 1963)/*Nine* (Marshall, 2009). These essays, essentially comparative in nature, shed light on the profound impact that Italian film has had on American cinema while underscoring the obvious and subtle differences that distinguish these two film cultures.

This brief history of the relationship between the cinemas of Italy and America outlines their interconnectedness, while the essays that follow detail specific examples of the exchange between the two film cultures. Although we cannot predict the future, it is safe to assume that Italian cinema, given its mastery of technique and appeal to American filmmakers, will continue to influence the production of film in the United States.

II

Screen Idols and Female Admirers in *The White Sheik* (Fellini, 1952), *The Purple Rose of Cairo* (Allen, 1985), and *Nurse Betty* (LaBute, 2000)

> "Italian movies were a great staple of our cultural diet. They were a tremendous influence in terms of showing us that one could make movies about mature subjects with profound themes."
>
> —Woody Allen, in an interview with Dave Itzkoff

At the American premier of *To Rome with Love* in June 2012, Woody Allen identified four films that have influenced his work: De Sica's *Ladri di biciclette/Bicycle Thieves* (1948) and *Sciuscià/Shoeshine* (1946), Antonioni's *Blow-Up* (1966), and Fellini's *Amarcord* (1973). The Italian directors, according to Allen, "invented a method of telling a story and suddenly for us lesser mortals it becomes all right to tell a story that way. We do our versions of them, never as shockingly innovative or brilliant as when the masters did them." Before the most recent and most obvious homage to Italian filmmaking in *To Rome with Love* (2012), Allen revealed his reverence for Fellini in a number of films. Early in *Annie Hall* (1977) an academic pontificates about Fellini's "indulgent" form of filmmaking (and misinterprets Marshall McLuhan's theories on media) while Alvy Singer (Woody Allen) and Annie Hall (Diane Keaton) wait in line to see *Face to Face* (1976), directed by Ingmar Bergman, the other major non-Italian influence on Allen's filmmaking. *Stardust Memories* (1980), Allen's interpretation of cinematic autobiography that borrows heavily from Fellini's *8½* (1963), is perhaps his most notable adaptation (and, unfortunately for the director, one of his least commercially successful films). In *Celebrity* (1998) Allen reinterprets *La dolce vita* (1960) in a distinctly American context that focuses on the contrasting fortunes of a divorced couple. This essay analyzes more subtle parallels between Allen's *The Purple Rose of Cairo* (1985) and Fellini's *Lo sceicco bianco/ The White Sheik* (1952). Both films reveal the profound impact of the fantastic, exotic figure of the screen idol on female viewers. By extension, Allen's undisputed influence on playwright and director Neil LaBute supports a reading of his *Nurse Betty* (2000) as a dark tale reminiscent of Fellini's *The White Sheik* that concludes more felicitously for its female protagonist in Italy.

In April 2012, speaking in Rome where his film premiered, Woody Allen described his latest work as a tribute to all the Italian films that had influenced him as a young artist. He said: "I grew up on Italian cinema. I have always been an enormous admirer of Italian cinema. Anything that appears in the movie that is redolent of Italian cinema is strictly something that I have absorbed through osmosis over the years and it comes out" (Pullella). Allen, who regularly attended screenings of film by De Sica, Rossellini, Antonioni, and Fellini in the 1950s while working as a stand-up comedian in Greenwich Village, acknowledges the import of those screenings on his filmmaking in *To Rome with Love*, with its Italian setting, actors, and language. One of the film's four nonintersecting subplots clearly follows the narrative of Fellini's *The White Sheik*, while others contain tropes that allude to the Italian director's other works. For example, media obsession with the quintessentially normal office worker Leopoldo Pisanello (Roberto Benigni) comments ironically on *La dolce vita* (1960), Fellini's film about celebrity and alienation during the economic boom in 1950s Italy. With that film, the word *paparazzo*, which derives from the surname of the photojournalist played by Walter Santesso, entered the international lexicon. In *La dolce vita*, Paparazzo and his sidekick, tabloid writer and protagonist Marcello Rubini (Marcello Mastroianni), frequent cafés and nightclubs on the fashionable Via Veneto, where one of the final scenes of Leopoldo's story takes place in *To Rome with Love*. Fellini's film focuses on stardom with Anita Ekberg's portrayal of Sylvia, an American actress who visits Rome. In Allen's movie, real Italian celebrities populate the screen: in addition to the appearance by superstar Roberto Benigni, Ornella Muti plays Pia Fusari, a film star whom Milly (Alessandra Mastronardi) recognizes, while heartthrob Riccardo Scamarcio plays the burglar who seduces Milly after the movie star Luca Salta (Antonio Albanese) leaves her in a luxury hotel room when his estranged and enraged wife arrives. Other characters in *To Rome with Love* comment directly on celebrity in the dialogue; for example, the chauffeur (Sergio Solli) notes the fleeting nature of stardom once Leopoldo is no longer wildly popular. Additionally, the religious procession that Jack (Jesse Eisenberg) encounters in Trastevere recalls the Fellinian trademark of parades that seemingly appear out of nowhere.

Meta-cinematic moments abound in *To Rome with Love*. Fellini is not the only Italian director whom Allen cites in this film that arguably features Rome as its protagonist, with piazzas, both imposing and quaint (Piazza Venezia, Piazza del Popolo, Piazza di Spagna, Santa Maria in Trastevere), fountains (Tartaruga, Trevi), and monuments both inside the city limits (Ara Pacis and Colosseum) and beyond (Tivoli's Villa d'Este and the aqueducts).[1] The careful observer of a rooftop party will notice a poster for Antonioni's *Red Desert* (1964), a dark tale of psychological pain and suffering set in the grim Ravenna winter, which is the antithesis of Allen's comedy and Fellini's *The White Sheik*. As the camera pans from the party where Jerry (Woody Allen) and Phyllis (Judy Davis), their daughter Hayley (Alison Pill), and her fiancé Michelangelo (Flavio Parenti) celebrate his father Giancarlo's (Fabio Armiliato) successful operatic debut, the poster announcing Antonioni's film appears inside the building. The connection between the two directors is not merely coincidental, for Antonioni had planned to transform his documentary about *fumetti* (illustrated photo novels), *L'amorosa menzogna/Lies of Love* (1949), into a feature film until illness prevented him from doing so. He sold the story to Carlo Ponti, who in turn gave it to Fellini (del Buono 7–8). The decision by Jerry, a retired impresario who specializes in unconventional operatic adaptations, to cast Giancarlo, complete with his shower stall, in *Pagliacci*, acknowledges the opera's author, Leoncavallo, as well as Franco Zeffirelli, who staged and directed the movie version of that opera in 1982. This operatic vignette performed by the internationally acclaimed tenor Armiliato, may also be a sly allusion to Fellini's *I Clowns*, a 1970 television movie in the form of a mockumentary about the director's childhood obsession with the circus.

To Rome with Love, like Fellini's *The White Sheik* before it, focuses on the intersection of celebrity and infidelity. Allen acknowledges his indebtedness to Fellini's solo directorial debut when he explains the inspiration for *To Rome with Love*: "One of the films that I was thinking of was one of my favorite Fellini films, 'The White Sheik.'" He continues by describing the subconscious effect it has on him: "I love the film so much, that stuff creeps into your pores and you do it without even knowing you're doing it" (Toro). Striking similarities appear in the tale of two provincial honeymooners, Milly and Antonio (Alessandro Tiberi) in Allen's film and Ivan Cavalli (Leopoldo Trieste) and Wanda Giardino (Brunella Bovo) in Fellini's original, who come to Rome from the north and south, respectively. Both couples are obliged to spend time with the groom's formal and judgmental relatives, yet fail to do so because of a series of mishaps and strange encounters. A prostitute (Penélope Cruz in the role of Anna) figures more prominently in Allen's version than does Cabiria (played by Fellini's wife Giulietta Masina), whom Ivan meets by chance, alone at a fountain at night while desperately searching for his missing wife. We note that Masina's fleeting appearance in *The White Sheik* presaged her Oscar-winning role in Fellini's *Notti di Cabiria/Nights of Cabiria* (1957). Milly represents the irrational, naive fan of a matinee idol as she wonders what it would be like to kiss the star Luca Salta. Male stars in both Fellini's original (Alberto Sordi) and Allen's reincarnation (Antonio Albanese) defy the stereotypical romantic ideal in both their physical appearance and demeanor. The directors appear to comment on the absurdity of young women's infatuation with celebrity when they fall for pudgy, older, comic actors who are more ridiculous than sexy.

The title of Fellini's comedy immediately and ironically recalls an earlier cinematic sheik, the one immortalized by the great silent film actor Rudolph Valentino. Famous for his dark looks and European charm, Valentino played the exotic title role in *The Sheik* (1921) and both father and son in his final film, *The Son of the Sheik* (1926). Fellini's sheik offers a hilarious commentary on the iconic role with which Valentino, who embodied both sides of the Atlantic as an Italian immigrant and American celebrity, was forever associated. Following a career as a male dancer or gigolo,[2] Valentino became a movie sensation after first being cast in *The Four Horsemen of the Apocalypse* (1921). Married twice, and technically to both Jean Acker and Natacha Rambova (née Winifred Shaughnessy) for a short time, Valentino

Figure 2.1. Rudolph Valentino.

battled insinuations that he lacked virility. An opinion piece in July 1926 in the *Chicago Tribune* entitled "Pink Powder Puff" lamented the feminizing effect that "masculine cosmetics, sheiks, floppy pants, and slave bracelets" were having on once-manly men and concluded by blaming the superstar: "Rudy, the beautiful gardener's boy, is the prototype of the American male."[3] Thus Valentino embodied a great irony, for on-screen he made women swoon, while in real life he worried that others thought he was effeminate and cowardly. This fear persisted even as he lay dying in the hospital. Dead at the age of thirty-one from a ruptured ulcer and resulting peritonitis, Rudolph Valentino had not one, but two funerals—one in New York, where he died, and then another in California, where his body was laid to rest, as his most recent girlfriend, Pola Negri, claimed that the two had been engaged. Valentino's youthful demise assured his immortality in the world of cinema and beyond, as his body, especially now in death, retained a particular hold on fans across the country.[4]

Valentino's starring role in *The Sheik* (1921) features the exotic male as object of desire for female viewers. As this essay demonstrates, in films such as *The White Sheik, The Purple Rose of Cairo*, and the television show *Nurse Betty*, male stars offer their female viewers a means of transcending the mundane in much the same way that Valentino's character, Ahmed Ben Hassan, did. *The Sheik*, directed by George Melford, was based on the eponymous novel written in 1919 by Edith Maude Hull, the wife of a British farmer, which appeared the year after American women received the right to vote. This novel created a subgenre of smoldering desert romance that featured dark-skinned Arabs who kidnap adventuresome, but essentially reckless, white women. Female spectators could identify with the Englishwoman Diana, who, after initial protestations following her abduction, comes to love and adore her sheik. Valentino asserted that this type of relationship was what females wanted; he was quoted in the *Baltimore News* in October 1921 as saying that women, "whether they are feminists, suffragettes, or so-called new women, like to have a masterful man make them do things" (qtd. in Leider 171). Yet the star did not believe in violence; he favored romance, declaring a year later in *Photoplay*: "The cavemen method I abhor. Who could desire a woman taken by force? Who could gain any pleasure from loving or caressing a woman who did not give in return?" (qtd. in Leider 171–172). Valentino went on to explain that women hankered for flattery, innuendo, and subtlety, all of which were sorely lacking in the United States. American men remained less impressed with Valentino, perhaps resentful of his popularity with women all over the world. Referring to the star disparagingly as "Vaselino," journalists and commentators compared Valentino unfavorably to Douglas Fairbanks, the quintessential leading man of the day.

Fellini's amusing comedy of manners *The White Sheik* plays on the cultural stereotype of exotic seducer of meek housewives embodied by Rudolph Valentino. The film's title and the protagonist's wardrobe confirm that Fellini's sheik is a much lighter version of the dark idol. The director's penchant for revealing the seamy underbelly of show business exposes Fernando Rivoli as a foolish person who bears no resemblance to the suave character he plays. Introduced as he swings in a grove of trees near the set where the *fotoromanzo* (photo drama or photoplay) will be filmed, and swathed from head to toe in white, Fellini's sheik is a philanderer who cowers in the presence of his jealous and strong-bodied wife. Yet, as Risset (63) explains, however absurd he might appear to the viewer, this sheik conjures up an exotic world: "From under swinging white veils, a masculine figure, affirmative and adventurous, emerges. In a single instant, the Orient appears before us, an Orient that is not the desert but, rather, romantic and immediate. A joyous exoticism, in suspense, is produced, provoking a child's wonder at storytelling."

Played with comic genius by Fellini's close friend Alberto Sordi, Rivoli represents the glamorous lover to the newly-married Wanda. When the young couple arrives in Rome for a honeymoon orchestrated by Ivan, Wanda secretly visits the studios of her favorite *fotoromanzo* to deliver a portrait of Rivoli to the magazine's offices. Instead of following Ivan's carefully planned itinerary, including

Figure 2.2. Fernando Rivoli (Alberto Sordi) and Wanda (Brunella Bovo) in *The White Sheik*.

visits with numerous relatives to national monuments, the opera, and the Vatican, Wanda slips out of the hotel while pretending to take a bath and ends up spending most of her first day and night as a married woman in the company of strangers. At the nearby production office in Rome, the starstruck Wanda impresses and flatters the copywriter of the *fotoromanzo*, Signora Vellardi (Fanny Marchiò), with her verbatim recall of various episodes. Wanda tells the writer how she waits anxiously each week for the next installment of the *fotoromanzo* to arrive in her small, provincial town; only while reading the weekly alone in her room "incomincia la mia vera vita" ("my real life begins"). Wanda, who insists that "la vera vita è quella del sogno" ("the real world is the one of dreams"), agrees with Vellardi's declaration that "Bisogna rinchiudersi nel proprio io" ("One must withdraw into oneself"). After suggesting dialogue to Vellardi for the script she is writing, Wanda meekly protests before following the production crew twenty-six kilometers from Rome to Ostia in order to meet her sheik. She spies her idol as if in a dream as he swings high above her in the pine forest. The starstruck newlywed joins the rest of the cast on the beach after spending time with Rivoli at a seaside bar. She agrees to assume the role of Fatima, the sheik's love slave, and before shooting begins, lets Rivoli take her on a romantic sail. When his bossy and buxom wife, Rita (Gina Mascetti), viciously attacks her after the pair returns, Wanda awakens from her trance and realizes the absurdity of her situation—a naive girl from the provinces has become a character in a fictional romance on her actual honeymoon. Still in costume, Wanda hitches a ride to Rome while fending off advances from the lascivious driver. Upon her return to the Eternal City, seeing death as the only solution to her disgraced condition, Wanda throws herself into the Tiber. The next morning, Ivan retrieves his wife from the hospital, where she is recuperating from her attempted suicide, and they hasten to join the extended family to receive a papal blessing at the Vatican. There, Wanda, after proclaiming her innocence (Ivan also falsely attests to his after spending the night with the prostitute Cabiria), adoringly looks at her husband as they march swiftly and deliberately arm in arm into St. Peter's Square and exclaims: "Ivan, il mio sciecco bianco sei tu" ("Ivan, you are my white sheik"). As Ivan returns his bride's compliment with a smile, the viewer immediately understands the irony of this remark.

The White Sheik failed to rank in the top-three Italian films during the year of its release, and hence it was not screened at Cannes. Instead, Fellini presented his film in 1952 at the festival in Venice, where it was roundly booed. Typical runs of *The White Sheik* lasted a few days. Shot on site in and around Rome, including beach scenes at Fregene, this film hit a nerve with publishers of the *fotoromanzo* who, according to Sordi, were angry at Fellini for harpooning the very genre they promoted.[5] *The White Sheik* fared much better after its reissue by Cineriz in 1961 following the international success of Fellini's *La dolce vita* (del Buono 15).

With the small-town character of Wanda Cavalli, Fellini demonstrates the magical power of the essentially Italian literary phenomenon that mixed film and romance, the *fotoromanzo*. This genre was relatively new when Fellini chose to satirize it in *The White Sheik*. The first example of this Italian literary phenomenon, *Grand Hotel*, appeared as an illustrated magazine series in 1946. Intended initially as an episodic adventure novel for boys and young men, the *fotoromanzo* switched its focus to love stories as publishers sought to expand the target audience to include older adults and women. In addition to thematic changes, there were structural alterations as well, with static photographs replacing dynamic sketches as the *fotoromanzo* attempted to approximate the cinema and its stars. *Bolero Film*, which appeared in 1947, was the first weekly *fotoromanzo*; it was an immediate success that lasted until the 1970s.[6] Wanda attests to the popularity and impact of the genre when she declares that the weekly delivery of *The White Sheik* allows her to escape, however momentarily, the boredom of her small town. Fellini's film comments on the relationship between the *fotoromanzo* and film as it depicts the production of a scene on the beach. There, director, actors (including Wanda), extras, exotic animals, and onlookers come together to approximate movement through a series of static photographs. These individual frames form the pages of the *fotoromanzo* that Fellini animates in his film. He showcases and critiques his own work as a director by focusing on the work of his alter ego, the director of the *fotoromanzo*, who attempts to control an unruly group of actors and onlookers with his megaphone and stern demeanor.

Wanda succumbs to the glamour and the exoticism suggested by *The White Sheik* in the same way that women had fallen for images of Valentino's sheik on-screen. Offering an escape to women young

Figure 2.3. Shooting the *fotoromanzo* in *The White Sheik*.

and old, married and single alike, romantic stories liberate women from the ennui of daily life. As such, these narratives serve as a metaphor for cinema itself. Wanda's trancelike state in the presence of Fernando Rivoli resonates with the short story by Ada Negri titled "Cinematografo" ("The Movies") that appeared in *Corriere della Sera* on November 27, 1928. Negri's protagonist, a mousy young woman by the name of Bigia, regularly attended the cinema, sometimes two or three times a week, just like many people of her generation.[7] In the 1920s and 1930s, the price of admission to the movies was low enough to allow even the most meager wage earners to attend regularly. In Negri's tale, the poor, single office worker escapes her profoundly mundane existence at the cinema by identifying with the actors. Even when she is not at the movies, Bigia dreams of that world. Negri describes her protagonist, whose very name is as unremarkable as her appearance, thus:

> È una piccola dattilografa, più sui quaranta che sui trenta. Non svelta e furba come tant'altre della sua classe. Un pò ingobbita nelle spalle, veste invariabilmente di color grigio-ferro o marrone scuro, col feltrino ben calcato sulla fronte, a coprir d'ombra gli occhi quasi senza ciglia. S'è fatta anch'ella tagliare i capelli alla maschietta; ma solo perché, deboli e incollati alla cute quali sono, il codino di topo troppo sottile per esser fissato dalle forcine non le scenda più nel collo a farla vergognare. Le vesti corte non le stanno bene, la tradiscono, per via delle gambe troppo magre: sulle quali, specie alle caviglie, le calze fanno ostinatamente qualche piega; e non c'è nulla che imbruttisca una figura di donna, e la impoverisca, più delle calze che facciano piega sulle caviglie. (She's just a typist, closer to forty than to thirty, not quick and shrewd like so many other working-class women. She slouches a little, and invariably dresses in steel gray or dark brown, with a small felt hat pulled tightly down over her forehead so its shadow will cover her eyes and thin lashes. She's had her hair bobbed like other women, but only so her fine hair—so limp it seems pasted to her head and so thin her braided bun slides out of the hairpins—won't dangle down her neck anymore and embarrass her. Short dresses don't look good on her. They betray her skinny legs, with her nylons obstinately sagging, especially at the ankles. There's nothing that spoils a woman's appearance and makes her more homely than nylons that sag at the ankles.) (trans. Pickering-Iazzi 58)

We understand that for Bigia, like Wanda in Fellini's film, the glamorous world of celebrity offers momentary relief from the crushing monotony of the real world. Yet the transformative powers of the medium prove disastrous, fatal even, for Bigia when she leaves the theater, imagining herself as the lovelorn star whose suicide is thwarted at the last moment by her beloved hero. Negri's nondescript typist is not as fortunate as the flashy blonde she believes herself to be at the moment: no knight in shining armor appears to whisk her from harm's way as she throws herself in front of an approaching automobile. Viewing her crumpled body dressed in shabby clothes, bystanders wonder who she is, to which Negri's narrator responds: "Nessuno. Quasi nessuno. Una piccola dattilografa che viveva sola, e non aveva che una passione: il cinematografo." "No one. Not really anyone. Just a typist who lived alone and had only one passion—the movies" (trans. Pickering-Iazzi 62).

The plot of Woody Allen's *The Purple Rose of Cairo* mirrors that of *The White Sheik* in that a young wife's disappointment with a husband who is uninspiring at best and downright cruel at worst leads her, literally, into the celluloid world. Allen sets his dark comedy in the Depression, which informs the reality of his protagonist, Cecilia (Mia Farrow), a waitress married to the brutish, unfaithful, and abusive Monk (Danny Aiello). She finds her only escape at the movies, in particular in light romances such as the fictional film *The Purple Rose of Cairo*, which follows a group of socialites who travel to Egypt, where they befriend the explorer Tom Baxter (Jeff Daniels) and later invite him to visit them in New York. The flower of the title refers to the rose that the pharaoh had painted purple for his beloved wife, which now, as Tom explains, grows mysteriously in her tomb. After viewing the film five times, Cecilia is flabbergasted when Tom, intrigued by her repeated presence in the audience, literally breaks the fourth wall and steps out of the screen to meet his faithful fan. When news of the character's escape gets back to the movie studio, the producers send for Gil Shepherd (also Jeff Daniels), the actor who played Baxter, to get him back on the screen in order to save his career and the producers' livelihoods. In the end, the star and the character he created proclaim their love for Cecilia. The real man, actor Gil Shepherd, wins the girl and then abruptly leaves for Hollywood once Tom Baxter returns to the film.

Amusing and profoundly depressing at the same time, *The Purple Rose of Cairo* is one of Allen's personal favorites. When asked which of his films he would watch again, Allen said in an interview with Rachel Dodes in the *Wall Street Journal,* "There are a few of my films that I thought were better than others. 'Purple Rose [of Cairo]' came out better than some of the others." This film, like Fellini's before it, takes its name from the spectacle within rendering *The Purple Rose of Cairo,* like *The White Sheik,* a meditation on the cinematic world of the imagination. Based on a melodrama set in the 1930s, an era often referred to as the Golden Age of Hollywood, Allen's film comments on the age associated with the formation of the major studios, the establishment of the star system, technological advances in sound and color (the advent of the "talkies" occurred at the end of the 1920s), and the development of genres such as the musical, gangster film, and horror film. In these years, escapist fantasies were particularly attractive to Americans suffering from the effects of the Depression. Sets of elegant penthouse apartments with iconic white telephones, like the one that Cecilia spies when Tom Baxter takes her beyond the screen onto the set of the film within the film *The Purple Rose of Cairo,* bespoke the glamor of this age. In fact, Cecilia notes the powerful symbolism of this luxurious lifestyle when she tells him: "My whole life I dreamed of what it would be like on the other side of the screen." These emblems of wealth and beauty were incorporated into the *telefoni bianchi* (white telephones), Italian bourgeois comedies of manners typical of the 1930s and 1940s. The informed viewer can see a sly reference to the *telefoni bianchi* that inextricably links Italian and American cinemas of that era. Casadio (21), in his analysis of Italy's imitation of Hollywood in these films, points out that increased production of "sophisticated comedy" by Italians was a consequence of the Alfieri Law (1938), which forced the departure of the American studios from Italy.[8] The Hollywood ambiance, characterized by sumptuous sets, well-to-do protagonists with no visible means of support, easy divorces and high-society life, that was so different from the Mediterranean world, fascinated Italian viewers. Yet, as Casadio (21–22) indicates, one of the greatest discrepancies between these two film cultures was the lack of character actors, so critical to the Hollywood comedies, in Italy.

The Purple Rose of Cairo mirrors many of the thematic concerns found in Fellini's oeuvre in general, and in *The White Sheik* in particular. The Italian director reveals the decidedly unromantic and unattractive underbelly of performances and, by extension, of show business. In *Luci del varietà/Variety Lights* (1950), Fellini exposed the world of

Figure 2.4. On the set behind the screen in *The Purple Rose of Cairo*.

spectacle as decidedly unglamorous. That film, cowritten with Alberto Lattuada, follows the fortunes of a troupe of vaudeville performers and its impresario as they face the vicissitudes of their trade, including poor wages, questionable lodging, and the vagaries of star attraction. Woody Allen's characters in the film within the film, each of whom claims to be essential to the plot, remind viewers of the ensemble cast of Fellini's *Variety Lights*, a dysfunctional group that quibbles about whose role is most important. Fellini's later films, such as *La dolce vita* (1960), *Ginger and Fred* (1985), and *Intervista/Interview* (1987), also examine the world of show business. Allen's *The Purple Rose of Cairo* dissects cinema's attraction in much the same way that *The White Sheik* seeks to dispel myths about spectacles in general, and the world of celebrity, in this case that of the *fotoromanzo*, in particular. Characters in Allen's film within the film discuss the limitations of their imaginary world, trapped (except for Tom Baxter, who manages to cross the border from imagined to real life) behind the celluloid, literally pushing their faces up against it from the other side. They must repeat their performances over and over without variation. Thus we are not surprised when characters such as the Copacabana nightclub maître d' Arturo (Eugene Anthony) rejoice at their liberation from the constraints of the script. As Tom tells Cecilia, he wishes to leave the screen behind because "I want to love, to be free, to make my own choices." Tom attempts to learn about the real world, especially about the miracle of childbirth and religious faith, from the prostitutes he befriends after escaping from the screen. On the other hand, this character also admits that people in his imaginary world are consistent because they "don't disappoint, they're reliable" in comparison to the real people he meets on his furlough from the film world.

Woody Allen, even more so than Federico Fellini before him, expresses the limitations of his fictional characters. Tom Baxter, unlike the White Sheik, cannot really love Cecilia, for his knowledge of the past and present is limited to the script of *The Purple Rose of Cairo*. He can express all the necessary gentility toward a woman, Cecilia in this case, but he has no capacity to love. In this way, he diverges from Fernando Rivoli in *The White Sheik*, whose problem is that he loves too much in real life. His domineering wife's jealous outburst attests to this when he and his love slave Wanda disappear in a sailboat as the rest of the cast waits impatiently for them onshore.

Figure 2.5. Cecilia (Mia Farrow) at the movies in *The Purple Rose of Cairo*.

Gil Shepherd successfully convinces Cecilia to leave Tom for him by asking her: "Do you want to waste your time with a fictional person?" The notion of choice, which distinguishes humans from actors, permeates Allen's narrative. In the end, Cecilia chooses the real world, telling Tom that he will be fine because "things have a way of working out in your world." A member of the cast notes that it is as if the real characters want to be fictional and the fictional real. Yet actor Gil Shepherd tells character Tom Baxter, his own "creation," that one cannot learn to be real, just as one cannot learn to become a midget. The interplay between reality and fantasy strikes at the core of cinema, and the power of imagination in particular. As Roger Ebert points out in his review of *The Purple Rose of Cairo*, this film poses essential questions about moviegoing:

> "Purple Rose" is delightful from beginning to end, not only because of the clarity and charm with which Daniels and Farrow explore the problems of their characters, but also because the movie is so intelligent. It's not brainy or intellectual—no one in the whole movie speaks with more complexity than your average 1930s movie hero—but the movie is filled with wit and invention, and Allen trusts us to find the ironies, relish the contradictions, and figure things out for ourselves. While we do that, he makes us laugh and he makes us think, and when you get right down to it, forget about the fantasies; those are two of the most exciting things that could happen to anybody in a movie. The more you think about "The Purple Rose of Cairo," and about the movies, and about why you go to the movies, the deeper the damned thing gets.

What renders Allen's film so profound, like Fellini's work before it, is precisely the fact that the viewer, as Ebert says, must figure things out for himself or herself while thinking about the big questions that cinema poses. Allen challenges accepted notions of spectatorship when Tom Baxter looks out from the screen at Cecilia, thereby breaking the fourth wall. Film viewing is no longer one-way. Tom's gaze initiates a crisis when he dares to become more than an actor on screen. In *The Purple Rose of Cairo*, the reversal of the gaze creates a disturbing situation not only for the audience in the film, but also for those in

Hollywood who are concerned with keeping their creations behind the celluloid curtain. This radical shift underscores the play between real and imaginary that is at the root of filmmaking and spectatorship.

In the end, Allen's film offers no resolution for Cecilia. After Gil abandons her, she returns to the movie house where her remarkable encounter with the world of fantasy began. There, she watches Fred Astaire dancing with Ginger Rogers as he sings "Cheek to Cheek," an iconic Irving Berlin melody from the 1930s screwball comedy *Top Hat* (Sandrich, 1935).[9] Cecilia's life, like the film itself, has come full circle at the movies. Faced with no alternatives, she will most likely return to her boorish husband, Monk, after the movie, but she remains enamored of the idea of romance despite her own tragic experience with it. Cecilia is trapped by the 1930s female sensibility, in a loveless marriage with a cad. She, like Wanda, who returns to Ivan, her *"sceicco bianco,"* has no alternative. The future for both Wanda and Cecilia is bleak, most likely filled with long and unhappy marriages.

On a practical level, the lack of narrative closure in *The Purple Rose of Cairo* suggests the inevitability of a sequel or a subsequent episode (as with soap operas), yet it also signals an appreciation of the

Figure 2.6. Tom Baxter (Jeff Daniels) and Cecilia (Mia Farrow) in *The Purple Rose of Cairo*.

human condition in which problems remain unsolved. Allen expresses his ambivalence about whether films should challenge an audience or liberate it from daily worries in an interview in the *Wall Street Journal*:

> I've often thought that there's a movie in two film directors. One makes these confrontational films that deal with these problems. The other one makes strictly escapist material. Which one is making the bigger contribution? You are living this terrible life. It's hot. It's sunny. The summertime is awful. Life is miserable. You duck into the movie house. It's dark. It's cold. It's pleasurable. You watch Fred Astaire dance for an hour and a half. And it's great. You can go out and face life, based on the refreshment factor. If you see the confrontational film, you have a different experience and it seems more substantive but I am not sure it does as much for you as the refreshment. A couple of laughs, a couple of dance numbers, and you forget all that garbage for an hour and a half.

In the end, Allen reveals the disorientation that results from blurring the lines between fantasy and reality. Fellini also frankly portrayed the ambiguities and vicissitudes of life. He believed that film should not offer simplistic answers to the profound queries of life; thus his films, like life, lacked narrative closure. Fellini (*Fellini on Fellini* 150) explained his perspective:

> My films don't have what is called a final scene. The story never reaches its conclusion. Why? I think it depends on what I make of my characters . . . they cannot evolve in any way; and that's for another reason. I have no intention of moralizing, yet I feel that a film is more moral if it doesn't offer the audience the solution found by the character whose story is told. In other words, the man who has just seen a character sorting out his problems, or becoming good when he started off bad, finds himself in a much more comfortable situation.

In both Fellini's and Allen's comedies, the fictional world of cinema is a feminine domain. When Cecilia invites her vile husband,

Monk, to accompany her to the movies, he replies: "You like sitting through that crap." He, ironically, prefers another form of crap—the kind that he shoots with his buddies. Monk blames the movies for filling Cecilia's head with silly ideas. No wonder Tom Baxter dazzles her so; this explorer embodies the adventure and love that is missing in her gray, depressing life as a failed waitress married to a ne'er-do-well husband living in a sad apartment during miserable economic times. The cinema, which Cecilia frequents alone, provides an escape from this gritty existence. Similarly, a scene cut from Fellini's *The White Sheik* illustrates the gender divide inherent in escapist fantasies. The following conversation, deleted from the final screenplay, between Wanda and Marilena Vellardi underscores the difference between women and men, wives and husbands regarding the fantasy world of the *fotoromanzo*:

Wanda: "Mio marito non lo sa che sono qua. Lui non mi avrebbe mai accompagnata. . . . Dice che sono una sciocca."

Marilena: "Oh, ma *quant'è* delizioso tutto questo. (con forza) Ma lui è sciocco! . . . Avete sentito, ragazzi? Che bambina coraggiosa. È che spunto magnifico per un fotoromanzo!" (Fellini, *Lo sceicco bianco* 43)

Wanda: "My husband does not know that I am here. He would not have come along. . . . He says that I am a fool."

Marilena: "Oh, this is all so delicious. (Forcefully) But he's the fool. Did you hear that, boys? What a brave little girl. And what a wonderful idea for a photodrama!"

Lousy husbands lead women to fantastic worlds beyond the limits imposed by reality. These men reject the allure that cinema offers the female imagination. The same phenomenon is at play in Neil LaBute's *Nurse Betty* (2000). In many ways, character and actor Tom Baxter/Gil Shepherd resemble Dr. David Ravell and the actor who plays him, George McCord (Greg Kinnear), in *A Reason to Love*, the soap with which LaBute's dark comedy opens. *Nurse Betty*, like *The Purple Rose of Cairo*, portrays a hapless waitress who is mesmerized by the lives of imaginary others. In this case, Fellini's *fotoromanzo* has been replaced by *A Reason to Love*, a fictional American soap opera. Entranced by that show, Betty Sizemore (Renée Zellweger), like Wanda Cavalli, initiates a quest that takes her far from home: in the contemporary tale, Betty first follows David to Los Angeles, the epicenter of American film and television, after which she travels, alone, to Europe. As in the two films previously discussed, the hope of transcending a dull marriage disintegrates after the female protagonist enters a world of fantasy only to become disenchanted by it. LaBute, like Fellini, focuses on a traditionally female genre, in this case the soap opera, in an apparent critique of the fictional world of the small screen. *Nurse Betty* and *The White Sheik* both end in Rome, where the female protagonists renounce their matinee idols for decidedly different reasons: LaBute affirms a thoroughly modern and positive future for Betty, while Fellini projects an old-fashioned, perfunctory marriage for his heroine Wanda.

Like Fellini's *The White Sheik* and Allen's *The Purple Rose of Cairo*, LaBute's *Nurse Betty* tells the tale of one woman's search to meet her idol, Dr. David Ravell. Betty's love for soap operas not only serves an antidote to the effects of the trauma she suffers from witnessing her husband's execution, but it also saves her life. Her complete

Figure 2.7. Betty (Renée Zellweger) working at the Tip Top in *Nurse Betty*.

identification with the soap opera world occurs when Charlie (Morgan Freeman) and Wesley (Chris Rock) murder her husband, Del (Aaron Eckhart, LaBute's college friend). After Betty observes Del's brutal scalping undetected by the father-son murderers, she heads west to California to erase the mind-numbing memories of her past by literally searching for *A Reason to Love*. For Betty, the soap opera world is redemptive. Whereas the world of the fictional Loma Vista Hospital had offered her an escape from the crushing boredom of waitressing at the Tip Top and the demands of her philandering used-car salesman, Del, it now provides her with a raison d'être following his death.

When Betty views Del's murder through a crack in the door, an action that mirrors the voyeuristic gaze of the cinema, she does not scream. Instead, she resumes watching *A Reason to Love* and enters the world it represents as a result of post-traumatic stress. The action both on-screen and in Betty's dining room display treachery: on-screen, Chloe, an operating room nurse, throws herself at David Ravell, who rejects her because he's still grieving for his late wife, Leslie, while outside the room, Charlie and Wesley kill Del for cheating them on a drug deal. Later, on television, Chloe accuses David of

Figure 2.8. Betty (Renée Zellweger) with cut-out of Dr. David Ravell (Greg Kinnear) in *Nurse Betty*.

sexual harassment in an attempt to advance her beau Lonnie's medical career. Refusing her advances, David tells Chloe, "There's really something special out there for me," a refrain that Betty will come to appropriate. Frames of reference collide as Betty tells her friend Roy the reporter in the aftermath that she "saw the whole thing; it was really disgusting," referring here to her new reality, Chloe's false claim of sexual harassment against David, and not to the murder in her living room.

Nurse Betty, written by John C. Richards and James Flamberg, signals a number of departures for Neil LaBute, who until this production had directed only films he had penned. This film had a relatively large budget ($24 million) compared with that of the director's previous project, *In the Company of Men* ($25,000). It was also the first time LaBute worked with major stars such as Renée Zellweger, Morgan Freeman, and Chris Rock. The number of scenes in this film was fifteen times greater (154 scenes compared with 10 in his previous work); it also included an action sequence. Critics such as Bigsby (190) viewed a new direction in the director's oeuvre: "This was decidedly not the Neil LaBute of his own early films." When queried about the larger message in this film, LaBute responded: "Was I trying to say anything with the film? Make a comment about the way reality and fantasy can so easily bend to our will, or bend us to its will? Point out that sometimes we have to go a little crazy to find ourselves? Probably, but nobody'll listen to that crap. . ." (qtd. in *The Shooting Script* ix). One hears echoes of Tom Baxter's repeated line that he is off to a "madcap Manhattan weekend" with socialites he meets in the Egyptian tomb when LaBute describes *Nurse Betty* as "clever, and fun and swell and romantic and madcap and frightening and provocative" (*The Shooting Script* x) despite its decidedly dark message.

LaBute, who studied theater in college and briefly in graduate school, watched a lot of foreign films at home on the Public Broadcasting Service. In an interview with Gerald Peary, he said that he felt as if he had completed "a survey course of the greatest works of world cinema" and continued by saying that "I saw *La strada* early on, *The Seven Samurai*. *The 400 Blows* was a favorite. I'm as happy watching *La dolce vita* as any movie I've ever seen. Now, I'm a big fan of Woody Allen and the Coen Brothers" (qtd. in Bigsby 3). Like Fellini's love of the circus (and spectacle in general), LaBute's fondness for film was inculcated at an early age. John Lahr observed that the phenomenon experienced by the female protagonist in *Nurse Betty* was strikingly similar to that of the director, a playwright and early film buff who watched films instead of going to football games on the weekend. Lahr (21) notes the autobiographical elements in *Nurse Betty*: "In the film, Nurse Betty is spellbound and it struck me over the next hour that perhaps the purpose of this exercise for LaBute was to live, however briefly, in the exhilarating spell of the Hollywood system that had captivated him as an adolescent on those Friday nights." He (127) describes LaBute's conception of Betty as part of a cultural phenomenon:

> LaBute, however, approaches his central figure protagonist, diner waitress Betty Sizemore, not as a delusional figure, a person different from the normal, sane inhabitants of a solidly real world, but rather as a participant in a widespread cultural fantasy, one of the many devoted followers of a popular soap opera, *A Reason to Love*. This "soap" is important to Betty, as it is to many of the other characters here because her own life is so impoverished, lacking in any real romance or promise, thanks to her dead-end job, curtailed education (she claims a year in nursing school), and cheating, drug-dealing husband, Del. Her relationship to that fantasy vehicle is part of the film's larger commentary on how people find mechanisms for coping with a lack of possibility, for filling a "gaping void" in both the culture and their lives.

LaBute privileges the soap opera medium by opening the film with a scene from *A Reason to Love*, which simultaneously validates the small screen and challenges the viewer's perception of the larger screen. As the image of the surgical theater becomes grainier, we realize that this is an image from television, not film. Thus, from the outset, the viewer, like Betty, seems unable to distinguish between reality and its melodramatic representation in the soaps. The viewer sees the intersection of the two worlds as the boundaries between the small and large screens fade. LaBute frames this juxtaposition (and the uncertainty that it suggests) when he cuts to the Tip Top Restaurant, where Betty mechanically pours coffee into Charlie's cup while glued to the tube.

Laura Stempel Mumford notes that the blurring of private space, typically associated with the female narrative, and public space, most often associated with the male experience, occurs frequently in soap operas; this phenomenon connects home and workplace, stereotypical female and male spheres. The soap opera captivates its fans through an intense experience of voyeurism in the public domain that results in the viewer's identification with the characters. Betty's show, *A Reason to Love*, is a typical soap opera narrative in that it, like *General Hospital*, is set in the familiar workspace of a hospital. In addition, private actions, such as sexual liaisons, are viewed by the audience and may be discussed after the fact in public settings. Gross breaches of privacy in this genre allow viewers to experience vicariously the intimate details of their characters' lives as voyeuristic pleasure. Consider Chloe's claim of sexual harassment after she has lured the still-grieving David Ravell to a secluded parking spot in order to position her beau, Lonnie, for the top spot in the hospital. The purported assault occurs in an episode that Betty watches after her husband's murder but is revisited subsequently in a discussion between David and his superior. Just as Wanda sees herself as the sheik's slave Fatima and Cecilia becomes Tom's girlfriend, now Betty identifies completely with Leslie, David Ravell's late fiancée, following Del's death.

When Betty leaves town in the middle of the night after her husband's murder, townspeople offer various theories as to why she left and where she went. Her female friends suggest that perhaps she decided to travel to California to meet Dr. David Ravell, yet the men in town refuse to accept the idea that Betty would travel halfway across the country in search of a character from a soap opera. Their inability to comprehend the power of the television show on the female psyche is evidenced by critical remarks made throughout the film. Husband Del disparages soap opera viewers as "[p]eople with no lives who watch people with fake lives"; the local sheriff Eldon dismisses Betty's purported search for Ravell as "the dumbest thing that I've ever heard"; hit man Charlie declares that a soap opera idol would be beneath Betty and later expresses astonishment about his son's death on account of a "doctor, a fake doctor." Even George McCord, the actor who plays David Ravell, denigrates the source of his livelihood by berating Betty for being "a soap opera groupie" and suggests that she "get a fucking life." Only Wesley—who will reveal later his interest in soap operas—believes in the possibility of Betty's search for a fictional character, because, as he says, "The bitch is a fucking housewife. There is nothing beneath her." Women, on the other hand, affirm Betty's quest and recognize its importance, even if they do not share her enthusiasm for fictional characters. Betty's coworkers at the Tip Top, her friend Sue Ann, the bartender she meets at the Grand Canyon Café, and her California roommate Rosa all agree with Betty that "there's really something special out there" for her.

Betty's complete engagement in the world of fantasy, like that of Fellini's Wanda, offers a wealth of material to be exploited by the creators of the fictional world. Wanda and Betty help the creators of their fantasies—Marialena Vellardi and Lyla Branch (Allison Janney), respectively—achieve greater effect with their female readers. When Betty finally meets George McCord, the actor who plays David Ravell, she impresses him with what he believes is her acting ability. Betty, of course, does an excellent job because she believes what she says. Vellardi and Branch appreciate the attention to their writing and understand the value that such devoted female fans add to their scripts. In the case of the American soap opera writer, this exploitation continues even after Betty's collapse. Following that debacle in the studio, Branch forces David to beg for Betty's continued involvement in the show in order to save his own character, his television career, and, by extension, her job as scriptwriter.

Soap operas, like the *fotoromanzi* of Fellini's generation, are aimed at a female audience. In fact, one can view the *fotoromanzo* as the prototype of the soap opera. LaBute's film demonstrates the fatal consequences for men when they cross gender lines and become fans of this essentially female genre. Even though Charlie must find Betty, the only witness to Del's murder and the driver of the Buick LeSabre in which Del has hidden the illegal drugs, he falls in love with her, or at least with the idea of her. He dreams of waltzing with Betty when he follows her trail through the Grand Canyon; later, he applies aftershave before he meets her in California.[10] These behaviors seem even more bizarre when one considers that Charlie has already killed thirty-three people and that Betty should be his thirty-fourth victim. Instead, Charlie, like Betty, has come to love someone he barely knows: the two met briefly when she distractedly served him at the Tip Top on the day of Del's murder, he interviewed her grandparents in Oklahoma to determine her whereabouts, read and absconded with her diary, and carried several photographs of her on the journey across the country. In the end, this infatuation compromises Charlie's professionalism and his life. Wesley, who reveals himself as a fan of the soap opera only at the end of the movie, dies because he watches Jasmine, his favorite character in *A Reason to Love*, instead of guarding his captives, Rosa, Roy, and sheriff Eldon, all of whom have come to save Betty from harm. Wesley loses himself in the discussion of Jasmine's sexuality; he is stunned to learn from his captives that she is a lesbian, and they take advantage of his pique to overpower him. Both men die in the end, Wesley by a bullet from the cops and Charlie by his own hand. Ironically, the demise of these two men confirms the powerful potential of the soap opera to alter lives.

The White Sheik, *The Purple Rose of Cairo*, and *Nurse Betty* demonstrate that the most destabilizing experience for the female fan is her entrance into the fictional world that she adores. A crisis occurs when the magic of the screen ruptures to expose an unpleasant reality to the female protagonist. For Wanda, the spell is broken when Rivoli tries to seduce her while they are shooting scenes in which she plays his slave Fatima. She spurns his advances in the same way that Cecilia initially refuses Tom Baxter's kisses. Both women, after all, are married. Memories flood Betty when she awakens from her stupor on the set of *A Reason to Love*, where George has brought her for a cameo appearance. When Betty realizes where she is, she nearly collapses. These dream worlds quickly come apart as reality replaces illusions of romance.

LaBute's ending repudiates the classical format of the storybook romance (here, romantic comedy) that concludes with the marriage of the female protagonist. Her husband's death has liberated Betty from the bonds of marriage that constrain women. Feminist literary criticism helps us understand the precarious middle ground of womanhood that Betty, Cecilia, and Wanda inhabit. Annis Pratt points out that there are countless literary examples of young women who view maturity as a curse that inexorably brings them to marriage, childbirth, and the ultimate struggle for survival as individuals. In many literary texts, the young woman realizes the real limitations to her imagination that marriage portends. For this reason, it is no wonder that women view matrimony as a negative institution, associated with the archetypal patterns of trauma and enclosure. Relationships in the three films bear out Pratt's formula that loveless marriages (without children in each case) encourage women to seek romance in the land of fantasy.

The films under examination adhere to Pratt's reading of marriage in the following ways: marriage extinguishes possibilities for self-realization when overbearing husbands like Ivan, Monk, and Del seek to control their wives' every action; authority figures (here, husbands and other male figures) banish ideal lovers by refusing to believe in the transformative powers of the imagination in soap operas, *fotoromanzi*, or film; gothic villains become husbands, particularly in the case of sleazy Del, unfaithful and unemployed Monk, and less so with punctilious Ivan; and consciousness of self leads eventually to punishment and madness, as Wanda is committed to an asylum after attempting suicide when she realizes her foolishness, Betty becomes seriously disoriented on the set where George McCord calls her "fucking crazy," and Cecilia fares slightly better when she returns to the world of the imagination in the movie theater after Gil Shepherd leaves her to return to Hollywood without saying goodbye. In addition, while male characters have affairs—Del and his secretary fornicate in the office and Ivan and Monk spend time with prostitutes—female characters hanker chastely (and safely) after impossible lovers (Pratt 32).

These films depict quests or tales of maturation such as those found in the literary genre of *bildungsroman*. Male and female versions of this genre take opposite paths: the male version portrays the protagonist's struggle within society, while the female version reflects women's existence outside the confines of society. This makes the woman's initiation less a self-determined progression toward maturity than a regression from full participation in adult life. In the novel of development, according to Pratt, tensions develop between a woman's desires and society's prescriptions of proper behavior that force women to seek fulfillment elsewhere. Female frustration with the lack of possibilities in the real world results in full participation in the dream world of *fotoromanzi*, romantic comedies, and soap operas, as this chapter demonstrates.

The marriages that Fellini, Allen, and LaBute depict are far from happy. The viewer doubts Wanda when she announces that Ivan is her sheik, for this "happy end" resonates with the depressing unions depicted in Pietro Germi's later brilliant *commedie all'italiana* of the 1960s, *Divorzio all'italiana/Divorce Italian Style* (1962) and *Sedotta ed abbandonata/Seduced and Abandoned* (1964). On the other hand, murder has liberated Betty from Del (as it does for Michelle Pfeiffer's character Angela DeMarco in *Married to the* Mob, directed by Jonathan Demme, 1988), allowing her to marry George McCord. But Betty has changed. She tells her matinee idol that even though, as her friend says, he's a gorgeous human being, he's "still an asshole." LaBute's interpretation of the female search for happiness upends the classical romance by offering instead a thoroughly modern solution in which the heroine lives outside the constraints of the genre and of society. Betty is an individual responsible for her own destiny; she proves what Charlie tells her shortly before he kills himself:

"Betty, you don't need any man, you don't need anybody because you've got yourself."

"You don't need that doctor. You don't need that actor. You don't need any man. It's not the forties, honey. You don't need anybody. You've got yourself . . . and that's more than most people can say."

Whereas *The White Sheik* and *The Purple Rose of Cairo* appear to reaffirm the notion that a woman's place, however unhappy it may be, is in the home, at her husband's side, preserving the honor of the family, *Nurse Betty* offers another solution. Betty travels to Europe ("the" Europe, as the voice-over tells viewers), alone, without male company. Wanda returns to her husband, the only possibility available to her in the 1950s, as Cecilia presumably did as well for lack of other options in the 1930s United States. Betty chooses a different path. She now stands as both subject and object. No longer enamored of the character David Ravell or of the actor George McCord, Betty has become the subject of her own life's story as well as the object of others' attention, as the final scene in Rome so clearly demonstrates. At a café in Santa Maria in Trastevere (not at the Vatican, as the screenplay suggests, which would have furnished a neat parallel with the ending of *The White Sheik*), a waiter absentmindedly serves Betty coffee while transfixed by her character, Nurse Betty, on the television screen. This scene recalls the opening of the movie, but with a new twist: now, an older, male Italian waiter hankers after an American female soap star, Betty. Life can imitate art, as Betty's experience has shown. She is now free to live her life unfettered by the fantasy world of others; *A Reason to Love* has become a "reason to live."

The titles of two of these films—*Lo sceicco bianco* and *The Purple Rose of Cairo*—refer to the spectacle to which the female fan is devoted. Federico Fellini's treatment of the *fotoromanzo,* with its origins in Italy in the 1940s, and Woody Allen's representation of the American melodramas of the 1930s showcase the male idol, who is arguably not the protagonist of the film. On the other hand, Neil LaBute's film promises another perspective. Nurse Betty, whose name is the title, embodies stardom on screens both large and small. All three films comment on the world of romance and celebrity that these media offer women whose lives are anything but glamorous. Fellini, Allen, and LaBute allow their female protagonists to experience the reality of what had served so long as a fiction. Ultimately, they must return to the world they left behind as they move from acceptance (Wanda) to resignation (Cecilia), and, finally, to independence (Betty).

III

The Art Film Reconsidered

Blow-Up (Antonioni, 1966) and
Blow Out (De Palma, 1981)

What happens when an American director known for his violent, almost sadistic films decides to interpret the quintessential European art film? Brian De Palma answers that question with *Blow Out* (1981), an American political thriller that includes many of the critical elements of Michelangelo Antonioni's *Blow-Up* (1966). Antonioni's film secured a place in the history of cinema because of the questions it raised about photography and, by extension, cinematography. Long a favorite in courses on film, *Blow-Up* is essentially a meditation on film and the visual arts, as it follows a photographer's attempts to understand his work. This contemplation of photography leads naturally to an examination of the mechanics and limitations of filmmaking, the art of the moving image. At first, Antonioni's protagonist, Thomas[1] (David Hemmings), misreads his photographs of a distinguished, older man frolicking with an attractive, younger woman in the peaceful setting of a London park. He views those idyllic shots of lovers as an antidote to the depravity in his book of photographs of London's underbelly. Gradually, through an examination of visual cues, Thomas discovers that he inadvertently photographed a murder. *Blow-Up* reveals these misunderstood images as constituting the larger scheme of aggression in Thomas's postmodern world, the anarchic possibilities of art, and the artist's inability to understand his own work.

Blow-Up, with its self-reflexive focus, inconclusive narrative, authorial imprint, and techniques such as the jump cut that define it as an art film, was both a critical and a commercial success.[2] The

film engaged many directors as well as audiences in Italy and elsewhere. In the United States, *Blow-Up* spawned imitations by Italian
American directors Francis Ford Coppola (*The Conversation*, 1974)
and Brian De Palma (*Blow Out*, 1981). The film continues to resonate
more than thirty years later, both ironically in the initial scenes of the
Austin Powers comedy *The Spy Who Shagged Me* (Roach, 1999) and
seriously in David Chase's *Not Fade Away* (2012). Italian filmmaker
Gabriele Salvatores presents an interesting twist on Antonioni's theme
in the detective story *Quo vadis, baby?* (2005), a film that features a
female private investigator, Giorgia Cantini (Angela Baraldi), whose
voyeuristic gaze allows her to interpret videotapes that in turn reveal
the circumstances of her sister's suicide many years before. Salvatores'
title is a cinematic palimpsest of sorts that refers both to Marlon
Brando's pickup line in Bertolucci's *The Last Tango in Paris* (1972)
as well as to the title of Guazzoni's 1912 film *Quo vadis?*, which was
later remade by Mervyn LeRoy in 1951.

By focusing primarily on the different sensibilities in *Blow-Up*
and *Blow Out*, this essay analyzes, in both form and function, De
Palma's adaptation of Antonioni's contemplation of his own craft. My
investigation demonstrates how the films' protagonists embody their
respective artistic concerns: Antonioni's protagonist Thomas wishes to
expose the truth behind the image, while De Palma's protagonist Jack
Terry (John Travolta) seeks to reify political corruption and nefarious
activities by matching sound to image in the story of an affair between
an older man and a younger woman. When De Palma changed the
title of his film about the murder of a presidential candidate from
Personal Effects (the name of Jack Terry's sound studio) to *Blow Out*,
he knew that people would compare his work to Antonioni's. He
figured that "commercially it wouldn't make too much difference,
because *Blow-Up* came out in 1966 and audiences wouldn't be getting them confused" (Amata 75–76). This chapter moves beyond the
similarity of the films' titles to examine parallels as well as divergences
between Antonioni's original and De Palma's adaptation in terms of
narrative and genre.

Like Antonioni's work, De Palma's film explores the mechanics
of filmmaking from the outset. In the initial scene, the camera follows a murderous peeping Tom's gaze first into a college dormitory
and then into the women's bathroom. As the killer pulls back the
shower curtain, a naked young woman screams in a scene reminiscent

of Hitchcock's *Psycho*. Viewers realize only at the end of the sequence that they are watching a film within the film (*Coed Frenzy*) along with the sound editor Jack, who has been called in by Sam (Peter Boyden) to remedy the actress's unconvincing shriek of horror. Little does Jack realize that his quest to find the perfect substitute scream will lead to a real crime scene on a riverbank in De Palma's hometown of Philadelphia. That evening, as he records sounds of nature in a bucolic setting similar to the park in which Antonioni's Thomas happens upon the playful couple, Jack also documents a murder. Presidential hopeful Governor George McRyan (John Hoffmeister) dies when the tire of the car he is driving is shot, not blown out, as the title suggests. This causes it to swerve and plunge off a bridge into the Wissahickon Creek. Jack saves McRyan's companion, Sally Bedina (played by Nancy Allen, De Palma's wife at the time), from the submerged car, but he is unable to do the same for the governor. Immediately after the accident, the cover-up of the crime—and the truth—begins, for the governor's campaign does not want to unnecessarily hurt McRyan's grieving widow by revealing the presence of her husband's paramour that fateful night. It turns out that Sally, like Jane (Vanessa Redgrave) in *Blow-Up*, was part of the larger scheme. Her boss, Manny (Dennis Franz), photographed the "accident" in order to blackmail the governor into dropping out of the race. It is those pictures that Jack will cut out of the tabloid, animate, and merge with his soundtrack to prove that McRyan's death was not accidental. Along the way, Jack misses some obvious clues that fatally endanger his accomplice, Sally. The movie ends as it had begun, with a cry for help. Sally's real scream, as the evil assailant Burke (John Lithgow) garrotes her, now substitutes for the actress's pathetic whine in the same porno horror flick with which the film begins.

 Blow Out, like *Blow-Up*, emphasizes the gaze from the initial scenes; in this way, both films comment on the art of cinematography. Jack Terry, whom the viewer first sees in the screening room of the B-movie studio, shares many of the voyeuristic tendencies displayed by Thomas in *Blow-Up*. In fact, he smiles to himself when the couple on the bridge above the riverbank where he is recording sounds in the night calls him a peeping Tom.[3] Obviously, Jack's work in the pornography industry, like Thomas's work in the fashion world, objectifies women and hence supports this reading. De Palma's insistence on voyeurism has provoked feminist critics, who interpret the violence perpetrated on female characters, often prostitutes or porn stars, in his films as strongly misogynistic.[4] The opening scene of the film within the film, *Coed Frenzy*, appears as ironic self-commentary on this aspect of De Palma's work.

Thomas, Antonioni's protagonist, also interacts with women in an essentially voyeuristic way. His photo shoot with the fashion model Veruschka, which resembles a sexual encounter, concludes abruptly once Thomas has elicited the image he wants. He watches his neighbor Patricia (Sarah Miles) as she makes love to her husband, Bill (John Castle), and he demands sexual gratification from two young women as payment for photographing them. The power of the male gaze informs Thomas's dealings with Jane as well. She acknowledges the equation of looking and sex by unbuttoning her shirt in exchange for the compromising photographs he took in the park. These scenes call to mind Laura Mulvey's seminal essay in which she posits cinema as an essentially male instrument for the objectification of women. According to Mulvey, moviegoers mirror

Figure 3.1. Thomas (David Hemmings) photographs Veruschka in *Blow-Up*.

the male voyeur as they sit in the dark and watch naked, or partially clad, female bodies on the screen.[5]

Yet gender distinctions between male subject and female object erode as both films progress. In *Blow Out*, Jack Terry, like Thomas when he views the dead body in the park at night (where an ambiguous sound—the snap of a branch or the click of a camera or a gun—confirms that Thomas is not imagining things), worries that he is being watched. His preoccupation creates a sense of paranoia, a justifiable response in this political thriller. Thomas, on the other hand, focuses more on his own understanding of what has transpired rather than on who might have done what. When both Jack and Thomas return to find their studios ransacked, they understand how quickly the gaze, which they had controlled, can now be turned back on them. According to MacKinnon (185), De Palma's voyeuristic tendencies in the two films that preceded *Blow Out*, *Greetings* (1968) and *Hi, Mom!* (1969), reveal the blurring of gender in this phenomenon: "The world divides into peepers and peeped, the former largely male, the latter largely female, but, with the technology available, a peeper can become a peeped with ease." Yet a critical difference marks these two films, for in the end, the reversal of the gaze in *Blow-Up* causes the viewer to question his or her role as spectator, whereas no such internal challenge awaits the viewer at the end of *Blow Out*. Ultimately, De Palma's film focuses on unraveling the mystery behind the death of Governor McRyan, while Antonioni's film contemplates the mystery of perception.

Critics, including Tomasulo, Casetti, Rushing, and others, have noted De Palma's appreciation and imitation of Hitchcock's insistence on the gaze. The gaze becomes the subject in many of Hitchcock's film, including *Rear Window* (1954), *Vertigo* (1958), and *Marnie* (1964). This phenomenon results in a more inclusive contemplation of the art of cinematography that mirrors the audience's experience. According to MacKinnon (181): "Hitchcock's great contribution to the debate about specularity may be that everything he says about voyeurism within the diegesis can be taken beyond it to the unseen world of the cinema audience. Thus, he is commenting on the experience of cinema itself." De Palma adopts this sentiment with a literal embrace of Hitchcock, saying: "Some of the most powerful images in cinema are voyeuristic images, because that's so much what cinema does. I think this is why so few people really understand Hitchcock; they write about his preoccupation with guilt and other schematic things, but Hitchcock actually discovered some very important intrinsic relationships in cinema—what you might call the essence of the medium—and this enables him to use it to its full extent" (MacKinnon 208n).

In *Blow Out*, De Palma sought to educate his audience on one of the more esoteric or technical elements of filmmaking—sound— against the backdrop of events that shaped the political landscape of his time. De Palma's work reminds viewers of the amateur film shot by Zapruder on the knoll in Dallas that captured the Kennedy assassination as well as the imagination of those who saw a political conspiracy in this tragic event. *Blow Out* also evokes the fatal crash on Chappaquiddick in 1969 in which Mary Jo Kopechne drowned in a car driven by Senator Edward Kennedy. But here there's a twist: in De Palma's film, the politician dies while the paramour lives. The director fancies himself a detective in his interview with Jean Vallely (73) about *Blow Out*: "It goes back to my assassination-buff years and Watergate, and how things get covered up. It's about explanations that don't explain anything. I think it will be quite original. I don't think the audience is aware of the sound-effects process. At the same time, it'll be a detective thriller, you know, putting together all these clues." De Palma's insistence on sound effects also constitutes the basis of his critique of Francis Ford Coppola's *The Conversation* (1974). The director, while recognizing the connections between his film and that of Coppola, deems *The Conversation* unsuccessful: "Both pictures deal with a kind of technical way of finding out about a crime. You know, the use of very tools in order to solve a mystery. This was also done in *The Conversation*, which is very much a cheat because they re-read the line: they don't really use all those filters to pick the line out. Ultimately, they re-read what she said: it's a different reading. It's a very terrible cheat" (qtd. in Vallely 76). We note that De Palma's critique of Coppola calls into question the very tools of filmmaking on which *Blow Out* focuses.

Brian De Palma's *Blow Out* insists more on the detective genre than does Antonioni's earlier art film. While both stories involve murders and unknown assassins, the two investigations differ in their purpose and even their subject. Whereas Antonioni's protagonist participates in an existential search for self, De Palma's character becomes embroiled in a larger political drama that almost dwarfs him. Thomas conducts a private, not public, search for truth. He never seeks to prove the body's existence to others, as evidenced by his complete lack of interest in reporting the murder to the authorities. It is true that he wishes to tell his publisher Ron (Peter Bowles) of the discovery, but in the end, he seeks to understand and verify his own belief. Jack Terry's private investigation points to a conspiracy to cover up the facts; he cannot turn to the police, for they insist that Governor McRyan's death be treated as an accident. Jack does not engage in philosophical contemplation, like Thomas, but rather conducts a covert criminal investigation. A contributing factor for Jack's modus operandi lies in his past life as a sound technician who outfitted undercover policemen with recording devices. When Jack recounts the tale of an undercover policeman whose profuse sweating short circuited his wire and blew his cover, the viewer sees the events leading to the cop's death in a series of flashbacks. These unnerving scenes reveal one reason that Jack's investigation remains outside the official police channels, for real, not imagined, danger pervades *Blow Out*. After Sally agrees to help Jack, she fears for her safety, with good reason. Although Jack began his inquiry in private, he ultimately involves the media when he engages the help of his friend, newscaster Donahue (Curt May), to protect the evidence. Yet his real evidence, Sally, will disappear when the villain Burke lures her into a deadly trap by pretending to be Donahue after tapping her phone line. The media does not help unravel this crime, but rather simply reports on the Liberty Day celebration in Philadelphia that serves as a noisy, chaotic background for Sally's murder.[6]

The protagonists in *Blow-Up* and *Blow Out* mirror the directors' work as they put together their own montage of events they had witnessed. Both Jack and Thomas rely on technology to help them understand what they saw in person. In *Blow-Up*, Thomas's curiosity about the emotion behind the image represents the antithesis of his work as a fashion photographer, in which he manipulates the viewer's emotion through the austere, superficial photographic image. While Thomas views the film that he shot, which proved so dear to Jane, we watch him as he examines the expression on the young woman's face and then follows her gaze, while she is locked in an embrace with her older lover, to the wooded area of the park. This scene of bucolic love, which conceals and reveals a tale of treachery and betrayal, stands in marked contrast to the ones in which Thomas placed the models in contrived configurations to evoke a fashionably "cool" world. Typically

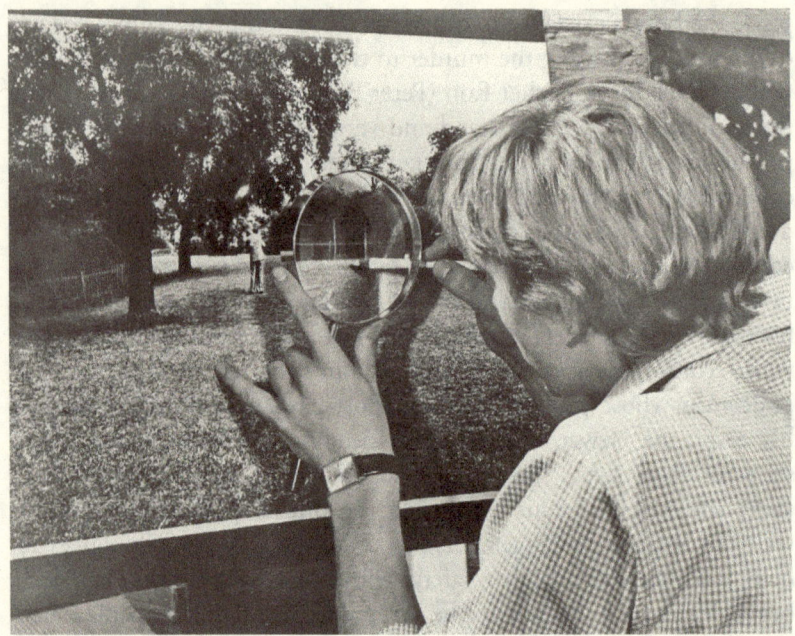

Figure 3.2. Thomas (David Hemmings) with his montage in *Blow-Up*.

he directs the subjects of his photographs, yet in the mysterious, unscripted sequence taken in the park, he feels compelled to do the reverse by unearthing the narrative and emotion behind the image. In this endeavor, Thomas acts as an amateur filmmaker whose gaze, shown by Antonioni's camera, enlivens the static photographs into a set of moving images through a series of jump cuts. In the act of filmmaking, Thomas discerns a truth that transcends his quotidian, fashionable world and eventually leads him to self-revelation.

As *Blow-Up* progresses, Thomas has more time to ponder what the characters in his own private film, caught in static photographs and reconfigured by his own enlargement and montage, might have done. In this way, the film within the film approximates a murder mystery in which Thomas acts as the detective. This whodunit, however, focuses not on the perpetrator of the crime, but rather on the witness who tries to figure out whether or not the crime actually happened. As his understanding of the scene develops, so does his comprehension of the nature of the day's events. We first hear Thomas tell his publisher that he has taken some beautiful, peaceful pictures in the park in order to blunt the sad facts of life that permeate the rest of his book.[7] He then calls to tell him that he saved a man's life by taking photographs—"This is fantastic, Ron. I saved a man's life"—only to realize ultimately that he had recorded a murder. Yet Ron does not show any interest when he hears Thomas announce, "Someone's been killed. I want you to see the corpse." His friend and publisher is in another reality, that of a marijuana-induced haze. Thomas will ponder the meaning of his montage alone; the private nature of this film within the film underscores and compounds his isolation in the world.

In *Blow Out*, Jack discovers the truth behind the film's title with help from Sally, and later from the newscaster Donahue, while Thomas works alone to realize the blowup (actually, an enlargement of an enlargement) of Antonioni's title. That image, in the context of the other enlargements, informs his montage of the events in the park. For De Palma's movie, sound is crucial. The director explained that the focus on sound came from listening to the anecdotes of many sound effects editors for years: "And I got to thinking, what would happen if somebody just by accident recorded a murder and what if someone else got a picture of it? If you sync up the two, I figured that you could actually see where the shot was coming from" (Amata 79). This is exactly what Jack does in *Blow Out*. The audience sees yet another film within the film as he synchronizes sound with images taken by Manny Karp, Sally's "colleague" of sorts. By focusing on the confluence of sight and sound, Jack realizes that the blowout was really a gunshot. Thomas's engagement with sound is more complicated. Whereas in *Blow Out*, Jack combines his recording of the blowout with the visual image in order to understand what happened when, in *Blow-Up*, Antonioni, not Thomas, adds the extra-diegetic sound of wind to his photographic montage to render the mini-film more realistic. At the end of Antonioni's film, sound creates further disequilibrium when Thomas hears an invisible tennis ball being batted about by mimes. This sound, which is disconcertedly part of the film's diegesis, underscores the photographer's inner quest while also challenging the viewer to contemplate its meaning, and by extension, the meaning of the film.

Both films closely identify the protagonists with their art. Thomas and Jack discover the truth of what they experienced outside—in

Figure 3.3. Jack Terry (John Travolta) in the sound studio in *Blow Out*.

Figure 3.4. Jack Terry (John Travolta) makes his movie in *Blow Out*.

the park and on the riverbank—in their studios, surrounded by the tools of their trade. Although they earn their livings in mundane jobs that objectify women—sound editing for porno flicks for Jack and fashion photography for Thomas—their real passions relate to different media. Whereas Jack collects sounds to enhance films, Thomas assembles images for his book. The viewer first meets Thomas as he returns from taking photographs in a London flophouse for his book on the violence of the city. When he hops into his Rolls-Royce, we understand that he has been masquerading as a poor person. Antonioni's viewfinder closely follows Thomas's camera, underscoring the importance of that object for his identity. The viewer meets Jack, who specializes in the recording of sounds such as wind, bodies falling, gunshots, screams, and glass breaking, at the screening of a pornographic movie that requires his expertise. His studio is an encyclopedia of sounds, now separated from their original contexts, which will become part of another film's diegesis. Following the accident, when the police try to convince Jack that his tapes do not prove the crime occurred and that he is imagining things, he defends himself by announcing his identity: "I'm a sound man!" Later, he will use his expertise with sound as way of ascertaining the truth.

Thomas's struggle to prove the existence of the dead body that he had photographed renders *Blow-Up* a meditation on perception. His attempt to discern reality from fiction directly involves the viewer, who, in turn, wants to know whether or not a murder occurred. Although Thomas has seen the body of the elderly man, both in the enlarged photographic image and on the ground, he cannot confirm the man's death because he does not have his camera when he enters the park that night. The next day, when he returns with his camera, the body is gone. Meanwhile, someone ransacks his studio and removes all photographic evidence of the body, except for one blurry enlargement, the "blow-up" to which the title alludes. The theft of Thomas's evidence underscores his alienation in a wider, violent and suspicious world about what really happened between the older man and younger woman. The magnified image proves nothing now that it is separated from the rest of Thomas's montage of that day in the park, just as one frame of a film may lose its meaning when removed from the larger narrative. As if to underscore the abstract quality of this enlargement, Patricia tells Thomas that it reminds her of one of her husband's art works, the meaning of which only becomes clear once he has finished painting. This lack of concrete proof forces Thomas to consider the essence of reality. Photography, which initially offers Thomas faith in his ability to create reality, now presents him with a paradox, for it both confirms reality through the act of reification and questions the objective notion of truth by creating an alternative reality that is beyond human perception. In fact, Thomas's gradual comprehension of what he saw in the park reflects Antonioni's analysis of the film: "*Blow-Up* is a film that lends itself to many interpretations because the issue behind it is precisely the appearance of reality. Therefore, everyone can think what he wants."[8] Jack, on the other hand, does not confront such existential questions. Having hidden a copy of his film in the ceiling tiles before his studio is burglarized, Jack preserves the proof, in sight and sound, that someone shot the governor's car tire. This evidence convinces the viewer as well of what happened, thus obviating the need to question our perception of the events.

Antonioni emphasizes the ineffability of his world by playing with the notion of truth in this film as he demonstrates its relative nature. Obvious allusions to the mutability of the "real world" occur throughout the film, notably in a confusing monologue in which Thomas tells Jane that his wife is on the telephone, then denies that she's his wife, saying they just live together, or rather that they just have kids together, only to retract the entire story in the end. Suggestions of spatial and temporal mutability abound in this film as when Jane, after an initial unsuccessful attempt at procuring the photographs, tells Thomas: "You've never seen me." When Thomas encounters Veruschka, the model whose birth name was Vera Gräfin von Lehndorff-Steinort, at a party in London the night he sees the body, he wonders why she is not in Paris as planned. Her response— "I am in Paris"—clearly is at odds with reality. In addition, Antonioni presents a number of altered states of perception, whether the drug-induced stupor of the pot party, the trancelike fixation of the nightclub goers, the models' dream state, or the fantasy world suggested by the mime troupe, which discombobulate the viewer. They also recall the narrative confusion, created by shifting viewpoints, of Julio Cortázar's short story, "Las babas del diablo"/"Devil's Drool," on which the film is based.[9]

De Palma's characters, whose actions are fixed in a definite time and place by television and radio reports simultaneously broadcast and shown on split screens, are more concerned with manipulating perceptions for practical and political purposes. There are no pot parties, rock concerts, or mimes to suggest an alternative reality in De Palma's film. Rather, as Bliss (101) points out, the viewer of *Blow Out* should pay attention to the clues found in the temporal and physical simultaneity of sound and image within the film, from the credits to the final shot. According to this critic, split screen images as well as television news reports in the background comment on the film's narrative and offer clues to the case that Jack often ignores. When campaign officials tell Jack that no one else was in the car when Governor McRyan drowned, Jack knows this to be untrue. Yet there is no underlying metaphysical problem here; only concern for the governor's political reputation and personal relationships erases Sally's presence in the car.

There are real differences in the films, for the violence suggested in Antonioni's film is shown in De Palma's. *Blow-Up* begins and ends with a troupe of mimes marauding through London. Thomas first meets them when returning home from the flophouse; he last sees them in the famous scene in the park, where they encourage his participation in their phantom tennis game. The stillness of the park scene as well as the peacefulness of the antiwar demonstration Thomas encounters on his way underscore the apparent tranquility of Antonioni's setting. *Blow Out*, on the other hand, begins and ends with the performance of violence on-screen in *Coed Frenzy*. De Palma's film concludes with a macabre twist as the fictional death on-screen becomes real. Life has imitated art in all its violence. According to Bliss (115–116), "*Blow Out* leaves us with the impression of a great soul's entrapment within a corrupt body, as fitting a metaphor for America as anyone in contemporary filmmaking is likely to give us for quite a while."[10] And Pauline Kael, who was much more complimentary of De Palma's film than she was of Antonioni's, appreciates the director's insistence on technique. In the *New Yorker* in July 1981, Kael praises *Blow Out* as

> the first movie in which De Palma has stripped away the cackle and the glee; this time he's not inviting you to laugh along with him. He's playing it straight, and asking you—trusting you—to respond. . . . When we see Jack surrounded by all the machinery that he tries to control

things with, De Palma seems to be giving it a last, long, wistful look. It's as if he'd finally understood what technique is for. This is the first film he has made about the things that really matter to him. "Blow Out" begins with a joke; by the end, the joke has been turned inside out. In a way, the movie is about accomplishing the one task set for the sound-effects man at the start: he has found a better scream. It's a great movie.

The titles of these two films offer a key to understanding the difference between the Italian film and the later American meditation on it. Both titles allude to underlying falsehoods: Antonioni's title refers to the photographic process that ultimately could not prove the truth, and De Palma's title comments ironically on what did not happen. *Blow-Up* concentrates on vision and its limitations; *Blow Out*, on the other hand, privileges hearing. Whereas the combination of sight and sound convinces Jack of the truth in his amateur film, for Thomas this confluence compounds the ambiguity of his situation. Antonioni concludes his film with sound questioning vision. When Thomas hears the bounce of the imaginary tennis ball in the final sequence, the effect startles the photographer and the viewer. The sound of something that clearly does not exist transports the investigation into an entirely new realm, past the tangible facts of "reality."[11] De Palma's film records no such belief in the ineffable, but rather remains firmly rooted in the prosaic and carnal, ending where it began with the dubbing of a pornographic film. We note the dichotomy between the art photographer, who captures images in the park, and the existentialist who deposits his camera to pick up the nonexistent tennis ball at the end of *Blow-Up*. No distinction exists for Jack who records the blowout and edits the porno horror film with Sally's scream.

If Jack Terry is a peeping Tom, the protagonist of *Blow-Up* recalls the doubting Thomas of the Gospels, the only apostle absent when the resurrected Christ appeared.[12] The parallel between Thomas the apostle and Thomas the photographer centers on both men's need to experience the truth. In this way, Thomas represents all who struggle with faith. Conversely, Thomas's questioning comments on the doubting Thomas's inability to believe without seeing; here the question ironically seems to be whether we can believe what we see. *Blow-Up* can be understood as a conversion narrative in which Thomas comes to an epiphany of sorts when he substitutes faith (belief) for perception as he watches, then hears, the nonexistent tennis ball. As I have argued elsewhere, Antonioni's film affirms the limits of vision, and the substitution of faith for the reality of photography.[13] What of De Palma's narrative? Jack Terry reaches no such epiphany. His use of Sally's real scream for the staged murder in the porno-horror film with which the film begins suggests perversion rather than conversion. Sally's disembodied cry, now coming from the land of the dead, represents, at best, Jack's attempt to reify the violence perpetrated against her and, at worst, a desecration of her life and, by extension, the value of his trade. Whereas Thomas's existential inquiry has transported him from the concrete realm of one-to-one representation of signified and signifier in order contemplate the nature of reality itself, Jack Terry's political investigation reduces his work to a scream in a porno film. Thomas, who literally disappears at the end of Antonioni's *Blow-Up*, veers toward the ineffable while Jack, who resumes his life where he left off before the murder, remains mired in the mundane in De Palma's *Blow Out*.

The Evolving Western

From America to Italy and Back in
Once Upon a Time in the West (Leone, 1968)
and *Kill Bill: Volumes 1 and 2*
(Tarantino, 2003 and 2004)

Throughout history, the notion of the West, as both a direction and a destination, has captivated writers and politicians alike as an outlet for imperialist conquests and pastoral yearnings. The Western film, as an embodiment of such expansionism, has exerted a powerful and storied impact on world cinema.[1] French critic André Bazin (140) views the history of the Western as almost identical to that of cinema itself, and the American scholar Jack Nachbar (2) deems the Western "the single most important story form of the twentieth century." The Western, which focuses on the places and philosophies that embody the frontier, resonates in a particular sense with its place of origin, the United States. The classical Western showcases the pursuit of civilization as the driving force of American frontier life, pushing societal mores onward into uncharted and therefore uncivilized lands. As Warshow (52) points out, the beauty of the Western lies in its consistency, because it is "an art form for connoisseurs, where the spectator derives his pleasure from the appreciation of minor variations within the working out of a pre-established order." Yet the enormous success, both critical and commercial, of the Western has inspired directors to adapt and translate its message in various genres, including, among others, horror, kung fu, and science fiction. Typical of the variety of these Western spinoffs are three recent releases from 2011: *Casa de mi padre,* a Spanish-language satire starring Will Ferrell and directed by Matt Piedmont; *Rango,* a comic Western in the form of an animated children's comedy directed by Gore Verbinski with Johnny Depp narrating the title role; and *Cowboys and Aliens,* a tale that begins in 1873 when a spaceship arrives in Arizona to take over the world, directed by Jon Favreau and starring Harrison Ford and Daniel Craig. Diverse adaptations such as these represent both a critique and an appreciation of the Western. They also signal its vitality.

The *western all'italiana* was a strikingly new interpretation of the Western when it appeared in the late 1950s and early 1960s as the American version declined in favor. The term "spaghetti Western," first coined by American critics of the Italian Western, reflected distaste for the European appropriation of this most American of genres (Frayling xi). In Italy, critics disparagingly called the films "macaroni" Westerns.[2] During the years between 1964 and 1974, approximately four hundred spaghetti Westerns were released; the highest volume per annum, seventy-two films, occurred in 1968, the year in which Sergio Leone released *C'era una volta il West / Once Upon a Time in the West* (Miccichè 114). During this period, European intellectual interest in the Western genre outstripped interest in the United States in this prototypical American genre (Cawelti *Six-Gun* 5). The spaghetti Western, in turn, affected American filmmaking and benefited actors in the United States. Cawelti ("Savagery" 115), for example, asserts that certain aspects of the spaghetti Western influenced John Wayne's "rugged individual" films. Most famously, Clint Eastwood, who was formerly known for his role in the television series *Rawhide,* returned triumphantly to Hollywood following his starring roles in Leone's successful *Dollars* trilogy, *A Fistful of Dollars* (1964), *For a Few Dollars More* (1965), and *The Good, the Bad and the Ugly* (1966).

Spaghetti Westerns parodied Western motifs and symbols in an attempt to subvert the traditional genre and, by extension, to criticize the American culture they represented. One of the main themes of what Frayling (xv) calls "both a celebration and a denunciation" of the Western concerned the notion of societal progress featured in the classical version. By exposing the violence on which such "progress" was predicated, the Italian interpretation of the Western differentiated itself from the *classico western americano.* In the traditional interpretation, violence occurs primarily as a consequence of the epic struggle between good and evil, justice and injustice, while in the spaghetti Western such violence, taken to the extreme, takes place outside such neat parameters. The spaghetti Western teems with all types of violence, including evisceration, blinding, scalping, slow roasting, and dismemberment, according to Miccichè (115).[3] Cawelti points out that in this world, "the moral man is the one who can use violence, treachery, and corruption most effectively" ("Savagery" 114). Thus, the representation of violence in the spaghetti Western differs from the classical interpretation that focuses on the construction of the epic, heroic representations of the past (Miccichè 115). Brunetta (*Storia* 780) sees the violence as a product of the era, which was characterized by "*una programmatica perdita del centro morale e ideale*" ("a systematic loss of the moral and ideal center"). The spaghetti Western's amorality reflects the destruction of taboos regarding the representation of death, as it alludes simultaneously through analogy and metaphor to the massacres of the same period, and to the Vietnam War in particular.[4]

Early critics of the spaghetti Western would be surprised by its continuing critical and popular appeal, as demonstrated by a recent retrospective on the genre held in June 2012 at Film Forum in New York City. This series, curated by Giulia D'Agnolo Vallan and Bruce Goldstein from public archives and private collections across Europe and the United States, featured works by masters such as Leone and Corbucci as well as those by less celebrated directors of the genre such as Giorgio Capitani, Damiano Damiani, Franco Solinas, Carlo Lizzani, Gianfranco Parolini, Sergio Sollima, and Tonino Valerii. Fans of what critic Bruce Bennett called a "uniquely violent and kinetic genre" attended screenings of major and minor works. This essay examines the ways in which the spaghetti Western, itself an interpretation of the classical Western genre, continues to influence American filmmaking, most notably in the works of Quentin Tarantino. An analysis of Leone's *Once Upon a Time in the West* and Tarantino's *Kill Bill* saga (Volumes 1 and 2) reveals how the European interpretation of the quintessential American genre informed subsequent Hollywood versions.[5] Tarantino, who proudly proclaims his appreciation of and admiration for Sergio Leone's art in his commentary on the DVD of *Once Upon a Time in the West,* employs extreme brutality in his own interpretation of the Western in *Kill Bill: Volumes 1* and *2* (2003, 2004). In this two-part series, the viewer notes similarities with Leone's subversive renderings of the American genre, which feature excessive violence and a powerful female protagonist.

Both Leone and Tarantino manipulate the classical interpretation of the Western, and with it the gender roles that dominate society. Sergio Leone's spaghetti Western *Once Upon a Time in the West* established a new paradigm by focusing on a lone woman, Jill McBain (Claudia Cardinale), as she navigated the male-dominated terrain of the West. As this chapter demonstrates, Tarantino's *Kill Bill* saga (which the director counts as one film) breaks new ground in his oeuvre by concentrating on one woman, Beatrix Kiddo, alias The Bride (Uma Thurman), in an attempt to seek revenge. Bill (David Carradine), the elusive male protagonist of the title, remains offscreen physically (with the exception of his hands, wrist, boots, and disembodied voice) in *Volume 1* and appears only at the conclusion of *Volume 2*. The Bride inhabits center stage. In the *Kill Bill* films, women, not men, perpetrate most of the violence. Although the roles typically associated with the Western are male—cowboys, Indians, good guys, bad guys, outlaws, sheriffs, and horse wranglers—Tarantino's film posits a new equation of women and arms. This chapter analyzes how Leone's and Tarantino's female protagonists, one through business, the other through violence, forge new codes of gendered behavior in these innovative treatments of the Western.

Once Upon a Time in the West, like other spaghetti Westerns, challenges accepted notions of progress, which are celebrated in the Western. In this film, Leone reveals the train, the engine that purports to civilize the wild, deserted lands, as a nefarious agent. He represents the railroad as a vehicle for greed and vengeance that brings destruction and degradation instead of progress to society. The film's opening scene at the station announces the connection between the engine and death. In a lethal land grab, the railroad baron Morton (Gabriele Ferzetti) sends henchman Frank (Henry Fonda) and his boys to annihilate the family of Brett McBain (Frank Wolff), the prescient owner of the seemingly desolate flatland known as Sweetwater. McBain had realized that his property contained the precious commodity of water, which is essential for both the men constructing the railway and for the steam engines that would travel on those tracks. Jill, Brett's new wife, whom he met and married in New Orleans, arrives to begin her new life in Sweetwater in the aftermath of the carnage. The mysterious Harmonica (Charles Bronson) and his sidekick, Cheyenne (Jason Robards), despite initial appearances to the contrary, help Jill outwit Frank, who now seeks to eliminate McBain's heir. As suspense builds and more cadavers fill the screen, Frank and Harmonica finally find themselves alone to duel to the death. In

Figure 4.1. Initial duel in *Once Upon a Time in the West* between Harmonica (Charles Bronson) and American guest stars.

the climactic encounter, heightened by Ennio Morricone's haunting score and Tonino Delli Colli's brilliant cinematography, which features 360-degree camera angles, Harmonica beats Frank to the draw and finally reveals the reason for his vendetta and the haunting flashbacks: Frank killed Harmonica's brother. The film concludes as the train arrives in Sweetwater, where Jill is now the station owner; Cheyenne dies and Harmonica rides away into the sunset, promising unconvincingly to return one day.

Another signifier of the Western, firearms, provides a matrix for the comparison of the classical Western and its Italian interpretation. In the classical Western, guns identify and define heroes. The spaghetti Western employ weapons, which are loaded with totemic value, in curious and surprising ways. A scene in *Once Upon a Time in the West* shows how a leg literally becomes an "arm" when Cheyenne, while riding precariously atop a railway car, places his gun in his boot and manages to liberate Harmonica from Morton's men by shooting them with this limb, which he dangles in front of the train window.

Guns lose a great deal of their symbolic and actual importance in the unabashedly capitalist society of the spaghetti Westerns. Frank's assertion, while gazing at a drawer full of cash in Morton's train, that dollars are more powerful than firearms embodies this new reality. By contrast, Harmonica, unaffected by capitalist greed, keeps his distance from money. In the deal to outbid Frank to buy Sweetwater, Harmonica offers up his buddy Cheyenne, on whose head there is a bounty. Yet there is no real exchange of cash and no real betrayal of his friend. Cheyenne, who has escaped from jail on numerous occasions in the past, most certainly will not spend a lot of time behind bars. After the auction, Frank offers Harmonica five thousand and one dollars to buy Sweetwater. Harmonica touches money for the first and only time in the film when he drops the dollar coin into a glass to pay for his drink. Harmonica's disinterest in financial deals marks him as an outsider in this new land where money motivates characters such as Morton, alias Mr. Choo Choo, who is determined to lay tracks all the way to the Pacific despite his physical disability; Frank, who dallies with the notion that money could replace guns; and Jill, who displays a keen determination to realize McBain's dream of building the station of Sweetwater.

The classical version and spaghetti Western diverge in terms of casting as well.[6] Leone selected iconographic actors for unorthodox roles to emphasize the difference between his interpretation of the genre and that of Hollywood. Instead of reinforcing rituals associated with the Western, familiar faces in unfamiliar roles underscore the manipulation of that genre. When Henry Fonda received a call from Leone about *Once Upon a Time in the West*, he assumed that he was being considered for the role of the good guy, as the actor explains in the extra materials on the DVD. Leone, who had other plans for the actor, asked him to return unshaven. Instead of playing his typical role as the smooth, handsome Western hero, Fonda assumed the role of cynical, sneering, villainous Frank. Charles Bronson, who started his film career (with his birth name Frank Buchinsky) as a renegade Indian warrior in *Drum Beat* (1954), plays the role of Harmonica, the mysterious and chivalric good guy with whom hazy flashbacks and haunting music are associated. The opening credits note that Woody Strode and Jack Elam, two iconic American actors of the Western tradition, are guest stars. Frank's hired guns appear on camera for the initial scene at the train station where they plan to kill Harmonica.

Figure 4.2. Harmonica (Charles Bronson) and Frank (Henry Fonda) working out a deal in *Once Upon a Time in the West.*

When he beats them to the draw, the viewer understands the American actors' abbreviated appearance as part of Leone's concerted effort to eliminate vestiges of the traditional Western in *Once Upon a Time in the West.*

Critics agree that Leone revolutionized the Western with his subversive approach to the genre, yet they fail to recognize his obvious critique of its traditional treatment of women. Certainly women play marginal roles in most Westerns; typically they are either bad (brassy saloon girls) or good (virginal daughters, virtuous wives, or schoolteachers). In his seminal article on the Western genre, Bazin (140-148) identifies the two women who vie for the hero's attention. According to the French critic, the hero meets an innocent young woman and the viewer believes that their love will be reciprocal. However, when the hero alienates the woman, he must convince her of his merit by saving her from imminent danger. Interference arises in the form of the other woman—a saloon girl—who also falls in love with the young hero. She will sacrifice her love and her life for the cowboy's salvation, thereby vindicating herself and satisfying the audience's expectations. French (62) echoes this interpretation and notes the expectations of censors to distinguish between good and evil: "In the model, traditional Western there are two kinds of women. On the one hand there is the unsullied pioneer heroine: virtuous wife, rancher's virginal daughter, schoolteacher, etc., on the other hand there is the saloon girl with her entourage of dancers. The former are in short supply, to be treated with respect and protected. The latter are reasonably plentiful, sexually available, and community property. There is obviously a correspondence between these two groups and historical actuality in the West—and an even greater connection between them and the orthodox thinking of late Victorian world. . . . The two classes of women also correspond, with the rewards and penalties their lives predict, to the demands of the Hollywood Production Code." Yet the spaghetti Western, which Ferrini calls the "anti-Western" because of the innovative ways in which it deals with elements such as firearms, figures representing the law, banks, duels, and animals, also posits a new reading of women in the West that distinguishes it from the traditional interpretation of the genre.

In *Once Upon a Time in the West*, Leone offers an alternative paradigm of womanhood by merging the distinctions of bad (former prostitute) and good (virtuous, grieving widow) into a single character, Jill. Indeed, her seductive appearance, which is enhanced by a Baroque hairstyle, exotic eye makeup, and revealing bodices, causes the (presumed male) spectator to want to see more of her. Whereas Bazin underlines the alterity of women in the Western, discussing them as instruments of male civilization, Leone suggests a more complex female symbolism. In keeping with his larger subversive premise, namely the explosion of the civilization myth of the Western, Leone reconsiders and revises the traditional role of woman as symbol of civilization. If in the traditional Western women stand at the center of the family, and the family stands at the center of the society, how do they function in Leone's film? The main female character in *Once Upon a Time in the West* does not fit the traditional model of woman as civilizing force, as Bazin (145) defined it: "The myth of the western illustrates, and both initiates and confirms woman in her role as vestal of the social virtues, of which this chaotic world is so greatly in need. Within her is concealed the physical future, and by way of the institution of the family to which she aspires as the root is drawn to the earth, its moral foundation." In the classical interpretation, the woman represents the voice of reason by speaking out against violence; her role as community builder is an extension of her maternal function. Yet in Leone's film there is no suggestion that Jill will remarry or have children. Whereas in the classical Western children perform a didactic function, providing adults with the possibility of passing on their wisdom to the next generation while reminding them of the innocence of childhood and underscoring the horror of adult violence (French 70), the abbreviated life span of the McBain children suggests the eclipse of childhood and perhaps the rise of the single, childless career woman (and powerful widow) in *Once Upon a Time in the West.* An altered society results in Leone's film, in which familiar bonds disintegrate and extrafamilial relationships develop (Cumbow 66). Instead of blood relatives, there are surrogate families predicated on friendship (Cheyenne, Harmonica, and Jill), or economic collaboration (Frank and Morton).[7]

Leone transforms the Western genre by investing extraordinary power in women. In an interview with Noël Simsolo (163), the director declares the end of the patriarchy in his new interpretation of the West. He posits a new matriarchal order in what he deemed a "pessimistic" film: "Avec *Il était une fois dans l'Ouest,* j'avais montré la naissance du matriarcat et l'arrivée d'un monde sans couilles." ("With *Once Upon a Time in the West* I have shown the birth of the matriarchy and the beginning of the world without balls.") The director's insistence on matriarchy suggests a new symbolic order. Jill's apparent lack of connections to male relatives—she appears to be no one's daughter and now no one's wife—emphasizes her alienation from a patriarchal society. Suddenly and prematurely widowed, Jill enjoys a masculine sort of independence because of her marital status. She is also a former prostitute, a figure whose power Warshow (46) identifies in the Western as "quasi-masculine independence" because "nobody owns her, nothing has to be explained to her, and she is not, like a virtuous woman, a 'value' that demands to be protected." When Cheyenne first meets Jill, he seems to intuitively understand her past, telling her: "You know Jill, you remind me of my mother. She was the biggest whore in Alameda and the finest woman that ever lived.

Whoever my father was, for an hour or for a month, he must have been a happy man." Jill, who tells Cheyenne ". . I don't look like a poor defenseless widow," realizes that she is not a valuable commodity in need of protection, but rather an independent businesswoman in control of her destiny no matter what violence men threaten, including rape.

On a superficial level, Jill appears to be the cinematic object of desire by male characters as well as by the presumed male audience. On-screen, all eyes focus on her singular beauty. When Jill enters the saloon on her way to the McBain homestead from the station, male customers and the proprietor alike stare at her. In another scene, following the successful barter of Cheyenne's bounty to secure the purchase of Sweetwater at auction, Harmonica goes upstairs and barges in on her as she takes a bath. There he comes face to face with what the camera suggests is the object of his desire (a beautiful, naked woman), yet other concerns distract him: in a perverse twist,

Figure 4.3. Jill (Claudia Cardinale) in *Once Upon a Time in the West*.

Harmonica saves Frank from an ambush by his own traitorous men, who had been bribed by Morton to kill their boss. These scenes present Jill as a more complex figure than mere sex object. In fact, sexual aloofness in the film distinguishes her from the archetypal showgirl found in the classical Western; this characteristic obliges the critic and the viewer alike to develop a new understanding of the female role in *Once Upon a Time in the West.*

One may ask why so little critical attention is paid to Jill, the only true female presence in the film and the one character whose narrative connects the two subplots of Harmonica and Frank. Leone underscores her association with water, which keeps man alive, fuels the steam engine (represented by the station of Sweetwater), purifies in the case of rape (as Jill tells Cheyenne), and restores (as in the bath she takes upstairs following the auction of her property). And critics readily acknowledge that Jill is the only person with a name who endures, who plays a role in the future of the West. Yet they do not see her as someone with whom the spectator, assumed to be male, identifies. Frayling (202) says of her: "Jill McBain is a reactor, a character who only makes sense, is only defined, with reference to the male protagonists. At least until the final sequence," yet grudgingly admits that Jill is "the only character who is not destroyed when history bursts in on the fiction: whereas the others play their parts, then bow out, she at last has a useful, purposeful role to fulfill when the railroad finally arrives. As the 'myths' dissolve, she comes into her own. Leone and Bertolucci may be misogynists but Jill McBain is the only one to survive." Cumbow (72) echoes this sentiment when he says: "Jill is the only person who survives; those who dig remain a faceless mass. The real personalities die or dissipate . . . numbers stand for people." Yet Jill's survival does not ensure her a place of importance with the critics.

Why do critics refuse to see Jill as a true protagonist in this film? Is it simply because she is female? When they consider her as only an object of male desire they ignore her importance to the narrative. Cheyenne's remark to Jill as the train crew finishes its work on the tracks at the end of the film illustrates this objectification: "If I were you, I'd go give those boys a drink. You can't know how good it makes a man feel to see a woman like you. . . . And if one of 'em should pat your behind. . . . make believe it's nothing. They earned it." The message is clear: Jill is an object without agency, a pleasure for us to consume with our eyes or for the railroad crew to touch with their hands. Cumbow (68) appears to have taken this suggestion seriously when, after acknowledging the importance of Cheyenne and Harmonica as well as "strong, but flexible people like Jill," he shifts recognition from the female protagonist to the male collective: "In the end, though, credit goes to the diggers (not to the heroes)—the Boys who built the West, the Boys who occasionally need a drink and the touch of a woman." Such critiques resonate with Budd Boetticher's rejection of female agency in film: "What counts is what the heroine provokes, or rather what she represents. She is the one, or rather the love or fear she inspires in the hero, or else the concern he feels for her, who makes him act the way he does. In herself the woman has not the slightest importance" (qtd. in Mulvey 750). French (67) appears to agree with this assumption, as he dismisses the female role in Westerns, with the exception of actresses such as Marlene Dietrich, Jean Arthur, Angie Dickinson, and Maureen O'Hara. He rejects the viability of female roles in these films: "Westerns of course have to feature women if only because commercial movies must offer some so-called romantic interest. When women take the centre of the stage in this most masculine of genres, the result is less likely to be a blow in favour of sexual equality than a strong whiff of erotic perversity." These assessments reveal that critics appear incapable of fathoming a strong female role in such an overtly macho genre.[8]

Cheyenne's suggestion that Jill share her body with those who "earned it" may extend beyond the railroad workers to the spectators of the film, who are assumedly male if we accept Mulvey's assertions about male spectatorship. Cheyenne presents Jill in the simplistic role of woman as object of male desire in the traditional Western, and, in fact, her exotic and voluptuous beauty suggests such an interpretation. Yet, I contend, the choice of Cardinale, a bombshell actress, should be reconsidered in light of the film's other casting reversals. If Charles Bronson and Henry Fonda play against type in this film, why would one assume a traditional role for Cardinale (who had already played the role of the independent-minded Maria in Richard Brooks's *The Professionals* in 1966)? While the actress's physical beauty evokes sensual pleasure, her character's entrepreneurial savvy and determination tell an entirely different story. Yet critics persist in applying a distinctly male perspective, asserting that there is no single character with whom the viewer can identify, as Cumbow (82) contends: "So we're left with Jill, the person to whom, indeed, our sympathies are most readily extended. But sympathy isn't the same thing as identification, and Jill certainly isn't the person we'd like to be or would leave the theater imitating or quoting." These male musings, with their disconsolate theme of a vague dissatisfaction, at once underscore and miss the point: the narrative points the viewer toward Jill, but she fails to satisfy, for she resolutely renounces any man who might in the course of the film serve as her "Jack."

The figure of Jill must also be appreciated as a challenge to the macho tradition of the Western. Leone's Jill is both bad girl (former prostitute) and good girl (McBain's widow); she is both subject and object in Leone's film. As subject she defines the action of the brave new world: Jill is an independent woman at the helm of a highly successful station town. Her future potential, economic and otherwise, on this new frontier could prove extraordinarily empowering for female viewers and, it seems, perplexing to male viewers. As object, Jill serves another purpose: her notable difference is a constant reminder of the threat of castration in this new "world without balls," in Leone's words. Mulvey (753), in her groundbreaking analysis of spectatorship, explains the threat provoked by sexual difference between the male viewer and the female subject on the screen: ". . the meaning of woman is sexual difference, the absence of the penis as visually ascertainable, the material evidence on which is based the castration complex essential for the organisation of entrance to the symbolic order and the law of the father. Thus the woman as icon, displayed for the gaze and enjoyment of men, the active controller of the look, always threatens to evoke the anxiety it originally signified."

Critics and viewers should adjust their perspectives accordingly when evaluating the female presence. Frayling (xv) himself recognizes that the spaghetti Western, as an example of "critical cinema," shocks the spectator into questioning what he or she is seeing and forces him or her to think about the film even after it is over. Yet this critic, like others, fails to extend this new critical vision to the interpretation of the woman's role in the spaghetti Western. It is time to recognize the import of Leone's statement about matriarchy and examine the traditions of machismo that have precluded a less sexist evaluation of this genre for too long. As Leone leaves the Western behind, he looks forward to the future with a new paradigm, at the center of which is his lone lady, Jill.

Leone's legacy appears in the works of Quentin Tarantino, whose adaptation of Enzo Castellari's macaroni combat comedy *Quel maladetto treno blindato/Inglorious Bastards* (1978) as *Inglourious Basterds* (2009), filmed in Italy, testifies to the American director's penchant for Italian film. Tarantino's latest film, *Django Unchained*, released in late December 2012, is loosely based on Sergio Corbucci's original *Django* (1966).[9] The film, which contains three songs composed by Ennio Morricone, begins with the liberation of Django (Jamie Foxx) by Dr. King Schultz (Christoph Waltz), a bounty hunter–cum-dentist who initially needs the slave's help identifying subjects. In the end, Dr. Schultz provides Django with crucial assistance in rescuing his wife, Broomhilda von Shaft (Kerry Washington), from the plantation owned by Calvin Candie (Leonardo DiCaprio). Tarantino's film also includes a cameo appearance by Franco Nero, who played the title role in Corbucci's earlier *Django*. When Amerigo Vessepi (Nero) meets the new Django character (Foxx) at Candie's ranch during a *mandingo* contest, he asks him to spell his name. Django complies, noting that the initial *D* is silent. Vessepi, who reflects Tarantino's predilection for altering the names of famous people (Vespucci in this case), responds that he knows not to pronounce the initial consonant. And well he should since he played Django almost fifty years earlier.

Tarantino's predilection for particularly brutal violence resembles that found in the films of Corbucci and Leone. In an interview with Gavin Edwards of the *New York Times*, Tarantino identifies violence as a defining theme of the spaghetti Western: "Any of the Western directors who had something to say created their own version of the West: Anthony Mann created a West that had room for the characters played by Jimmy Stewart and Gary Cooper; Sam Peckinpah had his own West; so did Sergio Leone. Sergio Corbucci did, too—but his West was the most violent, surreal and pitiless landscape of any director in the history of the genre. His characters roam a brutal, sadistic West." Although Corbucci addressed racism against Mexicans in *Django*, Tarantino decided to focus on slavery in his film because, as he wrote in the *New York Times*: "When you learn of the rules and practices of slavery, it was as violent as anything I could do—and absurd and bizarre. You can't believe it's happening, which is the nature of true surrealism."

One of the most eclectic directors in terms of influence, Tarantino cites other directors and films prodigiously. Menarini (105–106) notes the futility of cataloguing the elements from multiple genres that have influenced Tarantino's films. Perhaps, as Menarini suggests, the numerous citations of genre and other directors' work reflect the profoundly philological nature of Tarantino's oeuvre. Tarantino, who recalls watching foreign films as a youth, describes *Kill Bill* as a "duck press of all the grindhouse cinema."[10] In *The Guardian*, he identified the subconscious effect of watching foreign movies in theaters that offered mostly exploitation films:

> People didn't know that they were being fed a diet of foreign cinema, but they were. What was billed as *Teenage Enema Nurse* on the poster was a well-respected German sexual comedy that played in big cinemas in Germany. Or Spanish horror films—in America they would slap *The House That Vanished* or *Blood-Spattered Bride* on them and you think you're seeing a grungy movie and all of a suddenly, you see this terrific movie, lurid as hell, but really terrific.

Tarantino's *Kill Bill* series demonstrates the director's understanding of both Eastern traditions in *Volume 1* and Western traditions in *Volume 2*, according to Page (201). As such, McGee (236) notes, it represents a form of Western "appropriate to the age of globalization." The second volume of this saga owes much to the spaghetti Western in terms of tone and theme. In making *Kill Bill*, Tarantino liberally borrowed from *Hannie Caulder* (Kennedy, 1971), an imitation of Sergio Leone's spaghetti Westerns that was shot in Spain with British funding and American stars. Kennedy's "crafty little westerns" such as *Seven Men From Now* (1956) and *The Tall T* (1957), written for the director Budd Boetticher, had influenced Leone's film, according to Kehr (11), who explains Tarantino's attraction to *Hannie Caulder*: "[I]t's easy to see what pleased Mr. Tarantino in this tale of female revenge. Raquel Welch, at her tawniest, is the title character, a station manager's wife who has been raped by three bandit brothers (Ernest Borgnine, Strother Martin, and Jack Elam) and enlists the aid of a bookish bounty hunter (Robert Culp) to get her own back." In memorializing Leone and Corbucci (and others) at the end of *Kill Bill: Volume 2* with the inter-title "RIP," Tarantino overtly acknowledges his indebtedness to the masters of the spaghetti Western.

Like Leone, Tarantino knows the rules of filmmaking and its genres, and he revels in breaking them by casting Leonardo DiCaprio against type as the villainous Calvin Candie in *Django Unchained*, for example. As noted above, excessive violence directed at innocent victims such as women and children instead of gunslinging rivals, distinguished the spaghetti Western from its classical antecedent. Corbucci in fact appeared to predict the spaghetti Western's transformative powers on American directors such as Tarantino, whose savage, famously brutal productions include *Reservoir Dogs* (1992) and *Pulp Fiction* (1994), when he concluded decades earlier: "Our Westerns are more emotional and more realistic, but let's face it, they are also more perverse. There is everything: drugs, savage cruelty. We kill babies too. Soon the Americans will understand how things are. For the time being, they remain attached to honest fights and legal duels" (qtd. in Liehm 187).

The *Kill Bill* series diverges from those mostly male narratives in that it features women as the primary agents of violence. *Kill Bill* represents a shift in Tarantino's work from the "undeniable masculinity" of his two earlier films, *Reservoir Dogs* (1992) and *Pulp Fiction* (1994), according to Page (195), who says: "In *Kill Bill Vol. 1* there is no subtlety, but there is a growing predominance of female characters. All of the major characters in this film are women, apart from Bill, though whether you can truly count someone who might as well be playing the Invisible Man is a matter of opinion." In an interview with Rebecca Murray, Tarantino described the gender shift in *Kill Bill: Volume 1* at the time of its release: "This movie does not take place in the universe that we live in. In this world women are not the weaker sex. They have exactly the same predatory hunting instincts as the men, the same drive to kill or be killed." In the end of the two-part story, Beatrix realizes the title of the film saga when she kills Bill by employing a secret technique she learned from martial arts master Pai Mei (Chia Hui Liu). With the five-point palm exploding heart technique, she simultaneously hits five pressure points on Bill's chest, after which he takes five steps and then dies. Once a victim, Beatrix proves definitively that she is, as Bill says, a "natural born killer," despite the seemingly stereotypical role assigned to Beatrix by her nickname "The Bride." Conard (169) views gender roles in *Kill Bill* as deceptively transgressive when he states that "the film's apparent conservatism about gender may in fact represent the very enlightened view that, in those leading roles, the women in our lives were psychically (if not physically) deformed in their struggle to gain the power that they needed to perform those roles, the power which was their due." In *Kill Bill* Tarantino performs a cinematic Oedipal act through the double death of the father (of B.B. and of Beatrix, who tells her friends at the wedding chapel that her "father" Bill has arrived to give her away). As he eliminates film heroes, he replaces them with female action heroines such as Beatrix.

Kill Bill, like *Once Upon a Time in the West* before it, resonates with the notion of a failed union. The impossibility of marriage, as suggested by the mass murder at the chapel on which the saga is predicated, calls into question the supremacy of the traditional family. Both women lose their men: Frank kills Jill's husband before she reaches her new home, and Bill murders Beatrix's fiancé at the wedding rehearsal. Beatrix's nickname is ironic, for she, like Jill, is a bride without a husband, a woman whose attempt to celebrate unity ends in tragedy and the threat of death. Frank's suggestion that he might marry, not kill, Jill in order to get her property rights to Sweetwater, underscores the notion of women as chattel.[11] Despite, or perhaps because of, their lack of attachment to men, Jill and Beatrix survive. Whereas Jill is a solitary female presence whose enemies are male (Morton, Frank, and his men), Beatrix avenges both male and female attackers, in particular the mostly female DeVAS (Deadly Vipers Assassination Squad; the acronym itself is a corruption of the Italian expression for female star or diva, which derives from the word for female deity). Yet her ultimate and most intimate enemy is Bill, as the last scene of the film saga demonstrates. Jill defends herself, with the clever and unorthodox aid of Harmonica and Cheyenne, while Beatrix actively eliminates all in her path in action hero fashion. Beatrix literally takes matters into her own hands. Just as nobody owns Jill, certainly no one owns The Bride, who plans to marry Tommy Plympton (Christopher Allen Nelson) while very pregnant with Bill's child.

Both *Once Upon a Time in the West* and the *Kill Bill* movies are tales of revenge. As such, they fit loosely into Wright's classical

typology of the vengeance plot, itself a variation on the classical
Western plot, which reveals a divide between hero and society that
is no longer simple and straightforward (159). Whereas the classical
hero joins society because of his strength and society's weakness, the
vengeance hero leaves society for the exact same reason.[12] In Leone's
film, Harmonica seeks revenge for Frank's murder of his brother,
while in Tarantino's film Beatrix hunts down Bill and his assassins
for attempting to murder her along with the rest of the wedding
party. In *Once Upon a Time in the West*, Jill acts as the nexus between
Frank and Harmonica (in the tale of vengeance), while in *Kill Bill*,
Beatrix announces at the beginning of *Volume 2* that she is on a
"roaring rampage of revenge." Budd confirms this when he tells his
brother Bill: "That woman deserves her revenge. And we deserve to
die. Then again, so does she." Before her final encounter with Bill,
Beatrix eliminates other women, including O-Ren Ishii (Lucy Liu),
Sofie Fatale (Julie Dreyfus), Vernita Green (Vivica Fox), as well as
Elle Driver (Daryl Hannah). Disappointed to learn that Budd (Bill's
brother and the only other male member of the Deadly Vipers Assassination Squad, played by Michael Madsen) had buried her enemy
alive in a "Texas funeral," Elle claims that Beatrix "deserved better."
Shortly thereafter, Elle realizes her wish for a duel when Beatrix digs
her way out of the tomb and appears in Budd's trailer. The ensuing
tangle leaves Elle flailing blindly after Beatrix extracts her remaining
eye while the Black Mamba (a viper and also Beatrix's codename in
the DeVAS) prepares to attack. Elle's demise resonates with Dantean
contrapasso: she used the snake to eliminate Budd after procuring the
Hanzo sword that had belonged to Beatrix, whose name reminds
viewers of the Italian poet's muse. The final duel between Beatrix
and Bill, by contrast, is understated, chatty, and informal. When
compared to the solemn, highly choreographed, and almost balletic
encounter between Harmonic and Frank on the range, this longed-for
encounter appears almost mundane. The setting as well as the nature
of the fight is quite intimate. Beatrix kills Bill by literally and figuratively breaking his heart with the infamous five-point exploding heart
technique inside the hacienda where Bill has been living with their
daughter, B.B. (Perla Haney-Jardine). The shift in semiotic signifier
from the stereotypically male locus of the great outdoors of the Western (and Leone's *Once Upon a Time in the West)* to a stereotypically
female interior space in *Kill Bill: Volume 2* underscores the gender

shift in Tarantino's revenge tale. Furthermore, Beatrix celebrates the realization of the title of this film alone in the ignominious and highly personal space of the bathroom in the motel where she goes with B.B. after killing Bill.

Leone and Tarantino focus on the body of their female protagonists in significantly different ways. Whereas Leone's camera suggests voyeuristic pleasure through the shots of Jill's body as she lies with Frank or alone on her marriage bed early in the film, Tarantino's camera presents the body of his action heroine as much less of an object of desire. Jill unabashedly uses her body for sex, first as a prostitute for financial gain then as a woman desperate to escape her kidnapper (Frank). As Frank undresses his prey, he reminds Jill that she is embracing the man who killed her husband. Jill replies that she would do anything to save herself. This comment, like her profession in New Orleans, signals Jill's understanding of the economy of sex. Tarantino's Beatrix Kiddo uses her body as a defense mechanism in her quest to seek revenge and ultimately to recover her maternal rights. But she, unlike Jill, is not sexualized as a female presence on-screen; we follow Beatrix's moves more than her curves. Indeed, as action heroine, Beatrix emulates those empowered female film

Figure 4.4. Beatrix Kiddo (Uma Thurman) makes her moves in *Kill Bill Vol. 1*.

protagonists such as Sarah Connor (Linda Hamilton) in *The Termi-nator* (James Cameron, 1984), Ellen Ripley (Sigourney Weaver) in *Alien* (Ridley Scott, 1979), Yu Shu Lien (Michelle Yeoh) in *Crouching Tiger* (Ang Lee, 2000), and Trinity (Carrie-Anne Moss) in *Matrix* (Andy and Larry, now Lana Wachowski, 1999). Brown (49) suggests that the hybrid role played by the action heroine defies categorization for: "the action heroine does enact both masculinity and femininity. But rather than swapping a biological identity for a performative one, she personifies a *unity* (emphasis mine) of disparate traits in a single figure. She refutes any assumed belief in appropriate gender roles via an exaggerated use of those very roles." In this way, Beatrix reminds us of Jill, who also transcends the expectations of prescribed gender roles in *Once Upon a Time in the West.* In the end, for view-ers, Beatrix forges a new identity outside the usual parameters of gendered roles, just as Jill did before her. As Barlow (120) explains, Beatrix's attraction derives from the fact that "[s]he doesn't need to be judged by the standards of men or of women, but encompasses both, discarding the limiting trappings their culture has provided to each." She is not simply a cartoon figure, but rather someone who appeals to women because she transcends the role of male object of desire. This results in her special appeal, according to Barlow (122):

> The attraction, I think, is that Kiddo can fully realize her identity as a woman without assuming a feminine role defined exclusively by men. She doesn't have to become a dominatrix, for example, though she is an action hero. She doesn't have to flash her feminine attributes through scanty outfits or seductive behavior to somehow "counter" her toughness. Confident in her own being, she doesn't have to fight the sexism around her, defeating it instead through the essence of her own being, not by changing the signs of it or by seeing it through the actions or possessions of others.

Such a combination of male and female attributes results in Beatrix's empowerment. It also calls for alternatives to the binary treatment of male–female, good–bad, subject–object that has domi-nated gender film criticism in the past. Beatrix's agency moves beyond that of Leone's Jill, whose embodiment of the virtuous and licentious aspects of femininity failed to alter male critics' adherence to strict stereotypical expectations of the Western genre.

Beatrix's status as mother differentiates her from Jill. As noted before, in both Leone's spaghetti Western and Tarantino's postmodern Western, conventional families disappear and children seem particularly vulnerable. At the rehearsal dinner, Beatrix tells the preacher and his wife that her pregnancy will provide her with the family she currently lacks. She has deserted her other "family," Bill's posse of hired killers, the Deadly Viper Assassination Squad. After she learned that she was expecting a baby, Beatrix convinced Karen Kim (Helen Kim), whom Bill had sent her to assassinate, to avoid a shoot-out. Pregnancy ironically liberates her from the father of her child, as she tells Bill: "Before that strip turned blue, I was your woman. But once that strip turned blue, I could no longer do any of those things because I was going to be a mother." At the end of the *Kill Bill* saga, when Beatrix is finally reunited with her daughter, whose father she murdered, she rejoices at discovering her child alive. The message is clear: whereas this woman seeks motherhood, she does not need a man after conception. In fact, in the credits, Uma Thurman is identified as Beatrix Kiddo, The Bride, Black Mamba, and finally Mommy. Tarantino ends the film with an inter-title that underscores the matriarchal order of the animal kingdom that Beatrix and her daughter inhabit, which is decidedly not the wild West: "The lioness has rejoined her cub and all is right in the jungle." Here the director refers to the female of the species, whose specialized morphology (the lack of a thick mane) allows greater agility in hunting for the pride (from which male cubs are excluded at maturity). Tarantino emphasizes the centrality of the female protagonist who, like the lioness, will both kill her prey (Bill) and nurture her female cub (B.B.).

In *Kill Bill,* the father is unimportant. When Beatrix reclaims her maternity, she shows that the action heroine can have it all and live happily ever after without a man. Tarantino, like Leone before him, suggests a new symbolic matriarchal order, which Conard (168) explains thus: "What's more, Tarantino not only remakes this past according to this more mature perspective, but also according to his desires—Uma Thurman is not only his substitute mother and ideal actress, but also his dream lover (who didn't fall in love—or at least lust—with her, watching, say, *Henry and June*?). So, interestingly, despite its unreality, its storybook character, the film is a truer-to-life version of our childhoods than what most of us remember. The fathers are out as heroes; mothers have taken their place, as the central figures—struggling for power—we now recognize that they always were." Critical appreciation of the female role has come a long way since Leone portrayed Jill's role in the emerging matriarchy of the once-fabled West. In fact, it is possible to view Beatrix's happy realization, not repudiation, of maternity as part of a larger societal shift in attitude about women's roles from the early days of feminism in the 1960s to the post-feminist values of the new millennium.

Both *Kill Bill* and *Once Upon a Time in the West* are tales that attempt to retell history in fantastic or mythological terms. Leone's film engages directly with the myth of the Western; his title suggests that the West of the past is legendary, as in a fairy tale, and therefore no longer relevant to the contemporary world of the 1960s. The Italian director challenges both the cherished historical myths of the frontier as well as the genre that it represents by working outside Hollywood, literally and figuratively, but within one of its formulas. *Once Upon a Time in the West*'s mythic qualities and its insistence on memory and personal history (notably Harmonica's flashbacks to his brother's death by hanging at the hands of Frank) imbue it with a sense of the never-ending past in the present. Only in retrospect did it achieve recognition; only in the collective memory of film viewers and critics did this film about what life used to be like realize its potential. Upon completion of *Once Upon a Time in the West*, Leone announced his farewell to the genre:[13]

"I have finished, for the time being at least, with Westerns. I no longer love the things associated with the West as I used to—the horses, the firearms and so on. . ." (qtd. in Frayling 215).

Tarantino's *Kill Bill* films may also be read as a fable of sorts. As Barlow indicates in his application of Propp's morphology, these films comprise a fairy tale told through a variety of genres. In this saga, Tarantino offers a rereading of the films of Leone as well as those of other directors. Just as he had commented on the uses and abuses of cinema in *Inglourious Basterds*, with its film star, critic and movie-house manager working together to reverse the Nazi hold on filmmaking, in this film he offers critiques of other genres directly through his characters. Shortly before his death, Bill debunks "a staple of super hero mythology" by asserting that super heroes are born, not made by their costumes. He asserts that heroes such as Superman and Spiderman wear the clothing of everyday people (Clark Kent and Peter Benjamin Parker, respectively), not vice versa. Bill tells Beatrix that these weakling alter egos are "critiques on the whole human race, sort of like Beatrix Kiddo and Mrs. Tommy Plympton." As he attempts to eliminate the woman who would live a conventional married life, Bill ironically advocates for a new symbolic order that eliminates his own role. Beatrix, whose assumed name of Arlene Machiavelli suggests that she, like the Renaissance political theorist, believes that exercising one's power (even deadly force) may be justified to establish a new order.

Bill's theory suggests a new reading of the old story of male–female relations that applies to the critical reception of Tarantino's tale: we cannot ignore the centrality of Beatrix Kiddo, and if we do, Bill's last harangue will remind us that she is the heroine and not the housewife, the agent and not the object. With this film, Tarantino addresses, and indeed reverses, the inherent gender inequality in Hollywood that Scott ("Topsy Turvy" 44) describes as "a deep and ancient bias that underlies the way we talk about movies, and what we see in them—namely the assumption that stories about men are large, important and universal, while stories about women are particular, local and trivial."

Leone and Tarantino employ unorthodox elements in their critical narratives that question our preconceived notions of genre and gender. A radical change has occurred in the female role that allows for a new reading of women as agents of their own destiny. In Leone's film, which arguably focuses on Jill in a sustained way in a "world without balls," the female protagonist only once aims a rifle, while in Tarantino's film, Beatrix is a "natural born killer." Whether in Leone's reconfigured old West of the spaghetti Western or in the new West of Tarantino's action film, the female protagonist challenges accepted roles and mores. In doing so, she offers yet another hermeneutic for our understanding and appreciation of the ever-evolving Western.

Neorealism Revisited by African American Directors in the New Millennium

Precious: Based on the Novel "Push" by Sapphire
(Daniels, 2009), and *Miracle at St. Anna* (Lee, 2008)

> "I was always intrigued with European cinema, and hated most American cinema. I didn't like the one, two, three-*boom*! style, with a neat and tidy ending. That was never my scene."
>
> —Lee Daniels in an interview with Scott Foundas

Neorealism, perhaps the most distinctly Italian genre of filmmaking, emerged in the 1940s in the waning years of World War II in Italy. Representative of the Italian penchant for artistic expression and political commitment, this genre of filmmaking can be identified by its component parts as well as its narrative themes (Marcus, *Italian Film* 22). Characterized by the use of on-location shooting, long shots, natural lighting, nonprofessional actors, working-class protagonists, nonliterary dialogue, and open-ended narratives about World War II and its aftermath, this approach to filmmaking insists on the ethical aspects of representation. In his famous discourse on neorealism, Zavattini repeatedly used the adjective "moral" to describe this genre. A deep concern for the individual and the exigencies of daily life, indeed a belief in and appreciation for the fundamental primacy of mankind, underscored Zavattini's theory and practice as a screenwriter ("Some Ideas on Cinema"). The representation of antifascist political positions was essential to the works of other neorealist directors. Stylistically, neorealist films served as antidotes to the escapist tales of the bourgeois world of the *telefoni bianchi* (or middlebrow comedies called "white telephones," after the prop that came to embody Hollywood comedies of manners) that entertained the masses during the height of fascism. By combining the aesthetics of the documentary with the realism of contemporary Italy, neorealist films strove to tell compelling narratives about the individual and society. With their largely nonprofessional casts, these works, often hastily and crudely made due to the exigencies of the postwar period, sought to project objectivity (Marcus, *Italian Film* 22). The radical departure from the idealized world of traditional moviemaking in Hollywood productions and the bold handling of contemporary themes resulted in international acclaim for films such as *Roma città aperta/Rome Open City* (Rossellini, 1945) and *Ladri di biciclette/Bicycle Thieves* (De Sica, 1948).

From its inception, according to Brunetta, neorealism was an example of international cinema:

> Per qualche tempo il meridiano del cinema mondiale passa
> per *Roma città aperta* e da lì segna il tempo del cinema

Figure 5.1. Antonio (Lamberto Maggiorani) and Bruno (Enzo Staiola) Ricci contemplate a brighter future in *Bicycle Thieves*.

Figure 5.2. Pina (Anna Magnani) tries to defend her man in *Rome Open City*.

internazionale. Tra il 45–48 le opere di Rossellini, Zavattini–De Sica, DeSantis, Visconti, Germi, Castellani, Lattuada sprigionano con una forza di novità, un'energia e una potenza tali da cambiare le coordinate, i sistemi di riferimento, i paradigmi culturali, la prosodia, la sintassi e le poetiche di tutto il cinema mondiale. (For awhile the meridian of world cinema passes through *Rome Open City*, which marks the age of international cinema. From 1945–48 the works of Rossellini, Zavattini–De Sica, DeSantis, Visconti, Germi, Castellani, and Lattuada emitted an innovative force, an energy and a strength great enough to change the coordinates, systems of reference, cultural paradigms, prosody, syntax, and poetics of all world cinema.) (qtd. in Vitti 69)

Critics and students of Italian film celebrate this aesthetic movement despite the fact that it was rather short-lived and not necessarily successful in commercial terms. For reasons that this chapter addresses, neorealism continues to appeal to both directors and audiences outside Italy in the new millennium.[1] I contend that in the United States this genre of filmmaking informs the work of Lee Daniels and Spike Lee in particular. These two African American directors have signaled their knowledge of and respect for the neorealist masters Vittorio De Sica and Roberto Rossellini with both their words and their works.

The neorealist movement in film evolved from an earlier literary movement that had its roots in *verismo,* a late nineteenth century genre that was somewhat akin to, but different from, the French school of naturalism championed by Émile Zola and others. Reaching its height at the end of the nineteenth century and the beginning of the twentieth century, the verist movement included writers such as Giovanni Verga and Luigi Capuana who detailed the lives of working-class protagonists. Similar to *verismo,* neorealist fiction of the 1930s and 1940s portrayed simple life in a contemporary setting; the humanity and frankness of this prose stood in stark contrast to fascist propaganda that sought to portray Italy and the Italians in idealistic terms. Authors Elio Vittorini, Alberto Moravia, and Cesare Pavese adopted the neorealist literary style. Vittorini also embraced American literature as an antidote to the oppression suffered by writers in Italy during the fascist regime, as demonstrated by his work as editor and translator of *Americana* (1941), an idiosyncratic selection of American literature from the 1700s to the mid-twentieth century that included works by authors such as Melville, Twain, Poe, Saroyan, and Faulkner. For Vittorini, the translation of American authors represented a subversive force insofar as certain texts underscored the idea of the United States as both a place and a set of ideas that existed outside the constraints of fascism. As Delisle and Woodsworth (147) point out, "The myth of America, as a land embodying a harsh class struggle and at the same time utopian principles, posed a direct challenge to the fascist view of the world. It also fed quite directly into the postwar neorealist movement which was to have such a profound influence in Italian literary narrative and cinema."[2] Vittorini also wrote several novels, including his first and most famous, *Conversazioni in Sicilia/Conversations in Sicily* (1949), which begins with an introduction by Ernest Hemingway.

Luchino Visconti's *Ossessione/Obsession* (1943) offers an example of how neorealism functions in a cross-cultural context. Considered one of the first examples of this new aesthetic, Visconti's film was an adaptation of *The Postman Always Rings Twice* (1934), a detective novel by the American writer James M. Cain. That book inspired three other cinematic adaptations: *Le dernier tournant* by French director Pierre Chenal in 1939 and then versions by American directors Tay Garnett and Bob Rafelson in 1946 and 1981, respectively. Ironically, *Ossessione* was not distributed outside Italy until 1976 because Visconti had never obtained copyrights to the novel. According to Van Watson (177), this oversight allowed MGM to produce its 1946 version of the film. *Ossessione*, originally cleared by fascist censors, engendered vehement protests from Catholic clergymen. Later, at the urging of his son Vittorio, Benito Mussolini screened the film and allowed it to be shown with a few cuts. Although he purportedly despised Visconti's portrayal of Italy, Mussolini took a copy of *Ossessione* with him when he departed in haste for the Republic of Salò (Van Watson 177). Why did Visconti's debauched tale of unsavory, scheming, and unemployed characters satisfy fascist censors in the first place? Perhaps the fascist regime's fascination with, and respect for, Hollywood, which led Vittorio Mussolini to visit there in 1937 to work out a deal with producer Hal Roach, predisposed him positively toward this film. Italians had viewed a steady stream of American films until 1938, when their government decried a monopoly on the distribution of films by instituting a flat rate for movie imports. After that, major American studios ceased distribution to Italy because of the disadvantageous terms; a few independent American producers continued to export their products to Italy. Contrary to what fascist officials feared and predicted, Italian production increased to fill the void even though American film distribution had grown to such an extent that it represented between 75 and 80 percent of all films shown in Italy prior to the Alfieri Law of 1938. During this period, imitations of Hollywood films were particularly popular in Italy, according to Segrave (108) and Treveri Gennari (8).

The transposition of Cain's 1934 detective novel set on the California coast into Visconti's 1943 masterpiece of cinematic realism in the Po Valley necessitated significant changes. In the novel, a handsome drifter named Frank Chambers meets and quickly falls in love with beautiful Cora, the wife of Nick Papadakis, a Greek immigrant and successful restaurateur. The tale of deception, murder, and infidelity chronicles the initial attraction between Frank and Cora, the subsequent unraveling of the lovers' bond, and their eventual reunion before tragedy strikes. In Visconti's film, the protagonists Giovanna (Clara Calamai) and her lover Gino (Massimo Girotti) understand the economic reality of relationships. Practical considerations, not love, underlie the union between the attractive but penniless Giovanna and the financially secure older man Bragana (Juan de Landa). But lust compels the young wife and her lover Gino to attempt murder, then to separate, only to reunite and finally succeed in killing Bragana. Ironically, in the end, Gino, who is questioned but ultimately not charged with Bragana's death, is arrested for Giovanna's murder when she dies after he swerves to avoid a collision with a truck in a true accident.

Neorealism has exerted its influence internationally, as recent volumes edited by Ruberto and Wilson and by Giovacchini and Sklar demonstrate. However, this genre's relationship to American cinema is complicated. Cesare Zavattini, one of the founders of the movement, emphasized neorealism's underlying difference from American filmmaking, stating in 1953:

> The cinema's overwhelming desire to see, to analyse, its hunger for reality, is an act of concrete homage towards other people, towards what is happening and existing in the world. And, incidentally, it is what distinguishes "neorealism" from the American cinema.
>
> In fact, the American position is the antithesis of our own: while we are interested in the reality around us and want to know it directly, reality in American films is unnaturally filtered, "purified," and comes out at one or two removes. (51)

While there is no disputing Zavattini's contention about the distance from reality that characterizes mainstream American films, recent works by Lee Daniels and Spike Lee evidence an appreciation, indeed an appropriation, of neorealism. Both Daniels' *Precious* (2009) and Lee's *Miracle at St. Anna* (2008) focus in a particular way on the African American experience, both domestically and abroad, in the contemporary period and during World War II. These films mirror the two sides of neorealism that either celebrate the war against fascism, as in Rossellini's *Roma città aperta/Rome Open City* (1945), or offer a critique of postwar society, as in De Sica's *Sciuscià/Shoeshine* (1946), *Ladri di biciclette/Bicycle Thieves* (1948),[3] and *Umberto D.* (1952). In this chapter, I argue that *Precious* and *Miracle at St. Anna* follow the neorealist prescription of honoring humble people in their daily lives.

In his essay on neorealism, Zavattini notes that directors of this genre prefer the quotidian, the commonplace, instead of the extraordinary stuff of fables. Neorealist films offer few, if any, solutions to the trenchant problems facing society. Zavattini (55) insists that the artist should show reality, not give answers to questions. He explains the selection of poverty as a neorealist theme, stating: "We have begun with poverty for the simple reason that it is one of the most vital realities of our time, and I challenge anyone to prove the contrary." Arguing against the claim that there is too much emphasis on poverty in neorealist films, Zavattini declares that these films move beyond a superficial portrayal to include an analysis of the phenomenon. In his seminal article on *Bicycle Thieves*, Bazin described the genius of this film, which he described as "pure cinema": "No more actors, no more story, no more sets, which is to say that in the perfect aesthetic illusion of reality there is no more cinema" (60). The sense of authenticity found in neorealist films resonates with Daniels' aesthetic as a filmmaker. He explains that the realism of *Precious*, a tale of an illiterate teenaged mother and victim of incest, originated in his personal experience: "I think what made *Precious* so true is that, down to the wallpaper, I worked from a snapshot of the room that I grew up in, the hallway I grew up in. I knew exactly where the paint was going to chip from the wall." Speaking of his subsequent film, *The Paperboy* (2012), the director said: "[I]t's very much in the stark and plain, deliberately ramshackle and stripped down mode of *Precious*. I'm not just talking about the look of the movie, either. I'm talking about atmosphere, the corroded and even cruddy authenticity that says, 'this is a movie that doesn't pretty things up'" (Gleiberman). Daniels' realistic presentations are both unselfconscious and evocative of a certain time and place. The director's emphasis on authenticity separates his films from other Hollywood productions. Gleiberman, for example, notes that *The Help* (Taylor, 2011) "looks about as naturalistic as a kabuki performance" in comparison to Daniels' *The Paper Boy*.

With a narrative set in a specific time (1987) and place (Harlem), Lee Daniels' *Precious* follows the neorealist conceit of temporal and spatial grounding as its humble protagonists confront racism and crushing poverty. In this open-ended narrative of the quotidian, which Roger Ebert described as a "landscape of despair," Lee Daniels renders his protagonist's life in painstakingly genuine detail. He does not spare the viewer the emotional, physical, and sexual abuse, harsh language, unappetizing images of food and vomit, or physical degradation that Claireece Precious Jones (Gabourey "Gabby" Sidibe) confronts in her mother Mary's (Mo'Nique), walk-up apartment. In fact, the actors felt their environment acutely. Sidibe, an acting neophyte, enjoyed filming the fantasy sequences, because her makeup, hair, and clothing provided welcome relief from the blood, dirt, and leaves that covered her in many scenes (Ebert). Known for his unorthodox casting (for example, Mariah Carey as a dowdy social worker), Daniels sought an amateur for the title role in *Precious*. Five hundred young women answered the open casting call for the movie, at which Sidibe, who was in her mid-twenties, was chosen. She had heard about the role from her mother, Alice Tan Ridley, a subway performer who herself had been approached to audition for the role of Mary (Hirschberg).

Figure 5.3. Precious (Gabby Sidibe) in *Precious*.

Daniels' protagonists speak the language of their class in 1980s Harlem, in much the same way that De Sica's and other neorealist director's characters spoke the dialect of their place and social standing. Zavattini, who championed the use of dialect, asserted that formal language creates dissonance in these social critiques: "In our literary and spoken language, the synthetic constructions and the words themselves are always a little false" (60). Daniels' insistence on authenticity of language appears in Mary's expletive-laced screeds and the idiomatic language of Precious's classmates in the Each One Teach One alternative school, where she finally encounters a teacher who will help her learn to read and write. The director extends this aesthetic choice to the fantasy scene in which Precious and Mary converse in Italian. In that scene, mother and daughter recite their lines in Italian, a feat that was achieved after intense language training. Sidibe reported that Mo'Nique only got the words right when the cameras rolled (Kramer).

The use of Precious's voice-over narration reminds the viewer that this story is being told through the lens of a child, another element typical of neorealist cinema, according to Bazin (53–54). It is easy to forget that Precious, who has a baby and is pregnant with another, is only sixteen years old, struggling with illiteracy in junior high school. Her use of inventive spelling appears in the film's credits including, for example, a quote from Ken Keyes, Jr.: "EvrY-FIN is a gif of TH unvass" which translates into standard English as "Everything is a gift of the universe." The initial frames of the film establish Precious's struggle with written expression and thus its link to the novel by Sapphire (*Push*) on which the film is based. Even though the protagonist is a teenager, her writing resembles that of a first grade student. Indeed Precious is much younger developmentally than she appears.

Precious, like the neorealist films before it, offers no facile solutions to the entrenched problems facing its protagonists. While much of the publicity surrounding this film focuses on Precious's obesity, the tragic state of her life as an illiterate, impoverished victim of incest renders her weight much less significant. Abuse is at the center of this film; in fact, the director (Daniels), promoters (Oprah Winfrey and Tyler Perry), and star (Mo'Nique) all claim to have been victims of abuse by family members (Hirschberg). Liberation from her mother's apartment, the locus of her physical and sexual damage, offers Precious a sense of hope, yet the viewer cannot forget that she is a single mother of two children, one with Down's syndrome. Additionally, and tragically, her HIV-positive status in 1987 meant she would most certainly die from the disease. When, at the end of Daniels' film, Precious leaves the apartment in which she has been abused repeatedly to a start a new life with her two children the viewer sees little chance for reconciliation. In fact, the rupture of the mother and daughter bond is the only hope for Precious's future. The literary sequel to this story, Sapphire's novel *The Kid* (2011), continues the tragedy as it chronicles the life of Abdul Jones, Precious's second child, from age nine, when his mother dies, to young adulthood. His world appears even crueler than that of his mother, yet readers may be less sympathetic to his state than to hers, as Michiko Kakutani suggests. She states that because of Abdul's violent rages, perverse actions, and deranged thoughts, we may experience revulsion at his character.

De Sica articulated the idea that neorealist films depict the complexity of human nature in an essay titled "On Character": "When I make a picture I love all the characters, their vices and defects. My work is human work. There is always an excuse, even for the criminal. Humanity is a very deep mystery. . ." (29). Bazin (69) speaks of De Sica's "inexhaustible affection for his characters," pointing to the fact that not one character in *Bicycle Thieves* is unsympathetic, not even the thief himself. Daniels appears to echo the neorealist belief in the complexity of the individual. When asked at the New York Film Festival if his intention was to disparage inner-city dwellers, he replied: "Even the most evil person was somebody's baby at one time. And that's where life is lived. I've never been that comfortable with black and white" (Hirschberg). Reviews of *Precious* focus on the visceral impact of Daniels' brutally honest portrayal of a marginalized and dysfunctional African American family. Writing in the *New York Times Magazine,* Hirschberg describes the reception of *Precious*: "[T]he audience's initial rejection of Precious, even repulsion at the sight of her, slowly gives way to a kind of identification." Hirschberg goes on to assert the potential universality of Daniels' title character: "Precious is a stand-in for anyone—black, white, male, female—who has ever been devalued or underestimated." In an interview in the *New*

York Times Magazine, Daniels underscores the simple truth behind our relationship to people like Precious: "People read so much into 'Precious.' But at the end, it's just this girl, and she's trying to live. I know this chick. You know her. But we just choose not to know her." This comment calls to mind Antonio Ricci, the hapless protagonist of De Sica's *Bicycle Thieves*, whose struggle to survive in postwar Italy was hardly unique.

Perhaps the most salient evidence of the influence of Italian filmmaking on Lee Daniels' work appears in his direct citation of De Sica's *La Ciociara/Two Women* (1960). Approximately halfway through Daniels' disturbing tale, De Sica's film appears on television as mother and daughter sit in the living room. *Two Women*, deemed a transitional film in De Sica's oeuvre by Marcus (*Filmmaking by the Book* 67) and others, signals a break with the director's neorealist past in several aspects. Vitti (294), for example, contends that this film represents "un melodramma concepito secondo le esigenze del divismo e le convinzioni della produzione hollywoodiana della grande specolarità" ("a melodrama born of the exigencies of the star system and the belief in Hollywood's epic-scale productions"). The appearance of this film within the film demands critical attention.

Two Women, like Daniels' film in which it appears, derives from a literary work that employs first-person narration. Alberto Moravia's highly autobiographical novel, *La Ciociara* (1957), draws on the author's eight-month period of hiding in Fondi, on the border of the Ciociaria, with his wife, Elsa Morante, following the declaration of the armistice on September 8, 1943. De Sica's close adaptation of the novel chronicles the experience of the widowed Cesira (Sophia Loren) and her teenaged daughter, Rosetta (Eleonora Brown), as they flee Rome, a city under bombardment, for the safety of their small hometown.[4] Once the Allies succeed in liberating the land from the fascists and the Germans, Cesira elects to return to Rome, where she had been the successful proprietress of a grocery store. Her decision to leave the safety of the group of refugees results in horrific violence. Cesira exhibits ferocious determination to protect her terrified child as the wild, animal-like French colonial troops known as Goumiers pursue both women inside the church in which they have sought refuge from the midday sun. After the vicious attack, Cesira awakens to see the open sky through the bombed-out roof, with swallows sweeping past. Tragically, the violence suffered by the two women reflects reality: historians recount that many Italian women were sexually assaulted by Allied troops, mostly North African colonial soldiers, following the final battles of Monte Cassino and the declaration of the armistice.[5] This attack also underscores the issue of race, for the soldiers are black and the women are white.

Critics of Daniels' film expressed skepticism that a poor, African American mother with little education living in Harlem in 1987 would watch a subtitled foreign film on television. The choice by Daniels, the first African American sole producer of an Academy Award–winning film (*Monster's Ball*, 2001), to cite De Sica's film highlights the Italian director's continuing significance for American filmmaking. Daniels, who was born a year after *Two Women* was released, unapologetically explains his selection thus: "Because I am watching 'Two Women,' and it's my movie. You're in my world!" (Kramer). Of the decision to include De Sica's film, he declared: "I thought it was so truthful—so in the moment" (Kramer). The parallels between the two film narratives go beyond Daniels' viewing fancy; they point to a deliberate selection that suggests the relevance of neorealism for films of the new millennium. *Two Women*, which, like *Precious*, focuses on marginalized female figures, makes a direct connection between Daniels' narrative and World War II. Considered by Moravia a paean to the Resistance fighters or *partigiani*, the novel on which the film is based can also be read as an example of neorealist prose. Faustini (286) reads the sexual violence perpetrated against mother and daughter as a metaphor for the evils of fascism that besieged Italy during those years. Moravia's novel, which was an expanded version of his earlier eponymous short story, was also the basis for Dino Risi's made-for-television film *La Ciociara/Running Away* (1988), also starring Sophia Loren.

When analyzed together, *Precious* and *Two Women* reveal disturbing parallels between the abusive conditions of Precious's life in the United States in the late 1980s and the deprivation and cruelty experienced by Cesira and Rosetta in the waning years of World War II when horrendous acts of violence threatened civil society. Precious, whose name ironically suggests that she is a treasure, shares a private hell with her antagonistic mother and, occasionally and tragically, with her abusive father. The challenges she faces—poverty, illiteracy, life-threatening illness, incest, single motherhood, raising a mentally handicapped child—are magnified in comparison with those encountered by Cesira and Rosetta. After all, Precious lives in the United States during a period of peace and relative economic prosperity more than forty years after the events portrayed in *Two Women*. This fact renders Precious's pain and alienation even more acute than the wartime suffering of De Sica's characters. As in many neorealist films, here also the protagonists are portrayed in relative isolation, with Mary and Precious often shown alone inside their apartment building. Yet unlike De Sica's neorealist critiques of postwar society in *Bicycle Thieves, Umberto D.,* or *Shoeshine,* Daniels' film demonstrates that institutions, and certain individuals within them, attempt to assist the less fortunate. Interventions by Precious's principal, Mrs. Lichenstein (Nealla Gordon), who comes to the apartment to tell Precious about alternative education at Each One Teach One, and later by her teacher, Ms. Rain (Paula Patton), make a difference in this young woman's life. Ms. Weiss (Mariah Carey), Precious's social worker, insists that her client tell the truth about her abuse in order to help her. There is no such assistance offered in De Sica's *Ladri di biciclette,* for example. In that film, trade unions, police forces, and the Catholic Church fail Antonio as he searches for his lost bike, as Marcus points out (*Italian Film* 64–65).

Other similarities emerge between the films in terms of the commodification of sex. In *Two Women,* the widowed Cesira decides to ask her married friend, Giovanni (Raf Vallone), to watch her store in Rome in order to escape the regular bombings. The unspoken understanding between the two suggests that he will take care of her store if she has sex with him, which she does. This compact tragically presages her daughter's decision to trade sex for stockings when the two women hitch a ride from a truck driver shortly after the brutal rape in the church. In *Precious,* children embody monetary compensation for sex. Mary receives benefits for Precious and her daughter Mongo (Quisha Powell), so named because she has the genetic mutation of mongolism, the pejorative term for Down's syndrome. Precious's mother also insists that her daughter seek social assistance instead of going to school, telling her to "get her ass down to the Welfare." Mary frames the discussion of such benefits in racial terms, declaring that "white folks get just as much or more state assistance than blacks."

In their Academy Award-winning roles, Sophia Loren and Mo'Nique portray mothers who have intense relationships with their daughters. At first glance, De Sica's film within Daniels' film suggests an antidote to Precious's abusive situation. Yet a more nuanced analysis reveals *Two Women* as profoundly disturbing for the mother-daughter dynamic. No doubt Cesira's ferocious defense of her daughter during the horrendous attack stands in stark contrast to Mary's lack of resistance to her daughter's rape by her own father. Yet Cesira's valiant effort ultimately fails. Careful consideration of De Sica's film narrative demonstrates the Italian mother's culpability of sorts: after all, her decision to leave the protection of the group of refugees to return to Rome after the surrender by the Axis powers led the two women to their darkest moment. In fact, both mothers, Mary and Cesira, do not or cannot prevent their daughters from being raped.

Precious's superficial examination of *Two Women* provides momentary solace, as her fantasy sequence demonstrates. Her complete identification with the daughter in De Sica's film occurs when she sutures herself into that narrative. This fantasy, like others in the film in which the protagonist imagines yearbook photos that speak

Figure 5.4. Precious (Gabby Sidibe) and Mary (Mo'Nique) at home with Mongo (Quisha Powell) in *Precious*.

Figure 5.5. Cesira (Sophia Loren) with Rosetta (Eleonora Brown) in *Two Women*.

and herself as a celebrity, represents a sanitized version of events in her life.[6] The imagined scene, which does not occur in De Sica's film, takes place in Italian around a table adjacent to the bombed-out church in which the pair have sought refuge. Here, Mary, as Cesira, encourages her daughter to eat in polite tones and mildly profane language ("Metti il culo sulla sedia" ["Sit your ass down on the chair"] or "Mangia, puttana" ["Eat, you whore"]) that pale in comparison to the vulgar expressions she hurls at her daughter in real life. In the fantasy sequence, the two women are dressed in the same clothing as the Italian actors. Their calm discussion of food contrasts with the crude and unappetizing exchange between mother and daughter when Mary insists that Precious eat, and then eat some more, despite her protestations. This bizarre form of punishment for not having prepared collard greens to accompany the pigs' feet ends with Mary telling Precious: "You fucked it up now you gonna eat it up."

Perhaps even more salient for this analysis of De Sica's influence on Daniels is the image that *Precious* and *Two Women* share: in these

Figure 5.6. Screen shot: Hole in ceiling in *Two Women*.

two films, a hole in the ceiling serves both as a technical device and as a metaphor for understanding the narrative. When Precious's ceiling breaks apart as her father rapes her, a fantasy begins, signaling an escape from the horrible violence. It is through daydreams such as this, in which she envisions herself as a celebrity, that Precious liberates herself from everyday violence. (The viewer notes Mary's shadowy figure in the doorway during the rape, suggesting the mother's acquiescence to this perverse act.[7]) In a voice-over early in the film, Precious declares her intention to survive: "I'm going to break through. I'm going to be normal." It appears as if the opening in the ceiling, which gives way to a scene of light and celebrity, promises Precious an escape from the violence and abuse that her father inflicts. Sadly, that is not the case.

Cesira and Rosetta focus on an opening in the ceiling as well. It is the last thing that Rosetta sees before her rape by the colonial

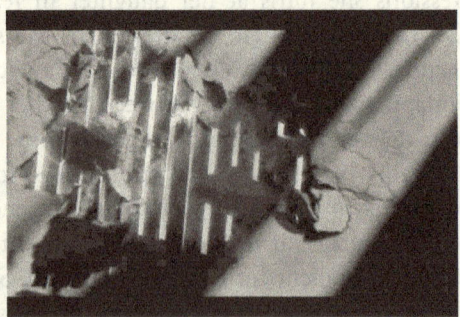

Figure 5.7. Screen shot: Hole in ceiling in *Precious*.

soldiers, and her mother finds her staring catatonically at it afterward. Thus, the two films are linked by a terrible irony: the image of freedom that promises Precious an escape into a fantasy world actually represents the aftermath of horrific sexual violence when we consider the meaning of the film within the film. The violence perpetrated against mother and daughter in a desperate, war-torn land in what should be a holy space (an abandoned church) finds parallels in the sexual abuse by Precious's father in what should be her sanctum, the home. Daniels does not present the violence depicted in De Sica's film, but rather makes a powerful commentary on the young woman's misguided fantasy. Precious fancies an escape into another world without grasping the entire narrative, and hence the terror, of De Sica's film. Nor does she comprehend the violence inflicted on Italian women after the Axis surrender that *Two Women* represents. Thus the film within Daniels' film underscores Precious's marginalized state: she cannot read the film nor grasp the historical events that inform its narrative.

In place of the horrifying rape that De Sica portrays, Daniels inserts a fantasy sequence in which mother and daughter reenact their previous conversation about food. This substitution signals Precious's desperate need to cancel her own memories of rape by her father and abuse by her mother. The hole in the narrative, filled with Precious's fantasy, constitutes an inherent irony. This metaphor for escape—a physical hole or a break in a story that can be filled with fantasy—is in fact a trap. As Marcus (*Filmmaking by the Book* 90) points out, in cinematic terms, this hole opens onto another plane, into a world beyond the confines of the camera. I would argue that the hole in the ceiling also establishes a dialogue of sorts between De Sica and Daniels in the same way that another famous literary opening, the chink in the wall through which Pyramus and Thisbe communicate, connects Shakespeare with classical mythology and, by extension, Ovid in *A Midsummer Night's Dream*. The reenactment of this tragic tale from antiquity permitted the sixteenth-century English playwright to comment on the forbidden love in his own comedy. As working men, the amateur players (or "rude mechanicals" as Puck calls Bottom and Flute and company) offer a contrast in terms of station to Theseus, Hippolyta, Egeus, the noblemen and women whose dramatic love story plays out on the larger stage. Precious's daydreams underscore the dissonance between her impoverished existence and the fabulous world of celebrity (the American alternative to royalty). The players' work, like Precious's fantasy, elicits questions about the use of imagination in life. Thus this opening is an appropriate metaphor for the conversation between the Italian and American directors Vittorio De Sica and Lee Daniels. Daniels' *Precious* owes much more to De Sica's filmmaking than the coincidental viewing the American director describes. Rather, as this analysis demonstrates, it is studied application of neorealist social critique.

Spike Lee employs the genre to expose racism at home and abroad in *Miracle at St. Anna* (2008). The director declared in an interview with the *Telegraph* that this film, which is a fictionalized retelling of an actual battle in the Italian campaign, "is a homage to Rossellini, De Sica, and those cats." *Miracle at St. Anna* signals a new direction for Lee whose earlier films such as *Do the Right Thing* (1989), *School Daze* (1988), and *Jungle Fever* (1991) addressed issues in contemporary black America. With this, his first work filmed outside the United States, Lee announced his intention to respect Italian history and not merely appropriate it: "We hope to get into Venice, and I think that the Italians feel this is their film. We're not just some American people coming over here and commandeering their subject matter."

More recently, another African American director, Anthony Hemingway, made his debut with *Red Tails* (2012), the story of Tuskegee Airmen, a segregated crew of black pilots during World War II. This film, which takes place in Italy and was filmed there as well as at Air Force bases in California and Prague, contrasts the acceptance by the native Italians of the Tuskegee Airmen (332nd Fighter Group and 477th Bombardment Group of US Army Air Corps) with the racism and condescension with which most of their white American commanders treat them. George Lucas had proposed initially that Lee Daniels direct the prequel to this movie and that Spike Lee direct its sequel. At a premiere of his film (and later on Jon Stewart's *The Daily Show*), Lucas told those assembled that he had financed this project, which had been in production for twenty-three years, because Hollywood would not back an expensive movie with an all-black cast. Lucas believed that it would not do well in foreign markets, which typically represent 60 percent of any film's profit.[8] This contention reflects a certain irony in that the black airmen in Hemingway's film, like the soldiers in *Miracle at St. Anna,* feel more at ease with Europeans than with their fellow white Americans. As Spike Lee points out, the same phenomenon occurred in the case of African American entertainers such as Josephine Baker, Miles Davis, and James Baldwin, who traveled abroad to seek freedom of artistic expression and refuge from the prejudice they experienced in the United States in the twentieth century.

Miracle at St. Anna contains several neorealist elements. The director tells his tale from the perspective of a child, a narrative strategy for which he thanks author James McBride on whose eponymous 2003 novel the film is based. McBride choose this viewpoint without realizing the importance of children in neorealist films such as *Bicycle Thieves, Rome Open City*, and *Paisan*. Lee sought an untrained actor for the role of Angelo Torancelli, the Italian youth who is befriended by the American troops. Like De Sica in *Bicycle Thieves*, Lee was searching for a child who had never acted before; he interviewed the top hundred of the five thousand children who showed up for an open casting call. In a conversation with author James McBride and Paul Holdengräber at the New York Public Library, Lee described Matteo Sciabordi, his choice for this role, as looking as if "he walked out of a De Sica or Rossellini film" ("Miracle at St. Anna"). Lee shot many other scenes on location, just as the neorealists did, and employed a crew of more than three hundred Italians. In order to preserve a sense of historical accuracy, Lee shot the scene of the massacre in the small Tuscan town of St. Anna di Stazzema in the actual spot where 560 innocent civilians, mostly elderly, women, and children, were killed by the retreating German SS troops on August 12, 1944. Queried as to why he chose to film in Italy, Lee quipped: "It took place in Italy" and later added, "You cannot duplicate the beauty of Tuscany with the mountains and hills" ("Miracle at St. Anna"). The director firmly believed that it was important for actors to speak their native language because that added a sense of authenticity to the film. He complained: "I'm tired of seeing war films where everyone speaks English, especially the Nazis" ("Miracle at St. Anna"). In addition, Lee hired an expert in military training, Billy Budd, to conduct a two-week boot camp for both the American and German soldiers so they would seem credible in their roles.

Miracle at St. Anna, like Lee's previous films, created controversy. Italians rejected the director's interpretation of the history of events that led to the massacre at St. Anna. In particular, they contested his representation of traitorous partisans who essentially delivered their fellow citizens to the advancing Nazis (Pisa). Lee attended the premiers of *Miracle at St. Anna* in Rome and Florence along with the main actors. When asked if he would continue making films in Italy, the director, who received Italian and French funding for the film with the stipulation that he find a domestic distributor (Disney Touchstone), responded that he needed a story to take him there ("Miracle at St. Anna").

Miracle at St. Anna follows the neorealist prescription of film as "moral imperative" or conduit for telling a forgotten or misrepresented chapter in history. The film recounts in flashback African American participation in World War II as a way of explaining the cold-blooded, seemingly random killing by the postal worker Hector Negron (Laz Alonso) in the initial scenes. As the narrative unfolds, Hector watches *The Longest Day* (Ken Annakin, Andrew Marton, Bernard Wicki, and Darryl F. Zanuck, 1962), starring John Wayne, which recounts the events of D-day from both the Allied and German perspectives, on television in his New York apartment in 1983. The Army veteran announces to no one in particular, "We fought that war, too." This scene introduces the theme of racial prejudice, experienced by African American soldiers during World War II, that the subsequent flashback will explore in greater depth.

Asserting, "There's no way that one film can eradicate the Hollywood omission of African American soldiers" ("Miracle at St. Anna"), Lee attempted to establish a memorial for the more than 1 million so-called "Buffalo Soldiers" of the 92nd Division and their wives. The original Buffalo Soldiers were organized in October 1917 for combat in World War I; their nickname derived from the name given by Native Americans to black cavalrymen during the Civil War. This segregated unit was the only African American infantry division to see combat in Europe during World War II.[9] As part of the 5th Army, the Buffalo Soldiers served in the Italian Campaign from 1944 to the war's end. Reports vary as to the reason for this name, but soldiers tell of wearing their insignia of a brown-black buffalo with pride.[10]

Lee's retelling of the story of the battles of the Serchio River, where many black soldiers lost their lives as white officers mistakenly sent firepower in their direction, was meant to reveal racism in the military. This difficult and prolonged battle, chronicled in detail by Hargrove (53–81), was one of the flashpoints for racial tensions in World War II. By resurrecting the memories of this division, Lee hoped to acknowledge the fine job that black soldiers, like James

McBride's stepfather and uncles, had done in the war. In an interview with Ty Burr of the *Boston Globe*, Lee recounted the connection between the black soldiers' return home and the rise of the civil rights movement. He added a critical scene at the soda fountain in the South that shows the deplorable treatment of black soldiers vis-à-vis German prisoners of war to highlight the unfairness of racial prejudice. Lee refers here to the Double V campaign which aimed to defeat both fascism abroad and discrimination at home, and the Jim Crow laws in particular. McBride's novel and Lee's film immortalize the sacrifices of black soldiers by recounting a formerly under-reported part of history, just as the neorealists had retold important events of the partisan participation in World War II. Author McBride in particular noted that without history there is no hope for the younger generation ("Miracle at St. Anna").

Neorealist directors also portrayed African American soldiers as Rossellini's *Paisà/Paisan* (1946) demonstrates. This episodic film, which chronicles the landing of American troops in Italy in the sum-

Figure 5.8. Spike Lee, wearing the Buffalo Solider insignia, on the set of *Miracle at St. Anna*.

mer of 1943 and their progress up the peninsula from Sicily to the Po Valley in the winter of 1944, focuses on the interaction of Americans and Italians, whether in battle, love, or friendship. American soldier and novelist Alfred Hays recalls the birth of this film, calling it "a rather casual parturition midwifed by a two or three bottles of vino dei castelli" at a Roman trattoria with Rossellini in the spring of 1945 as the war was ending. Hays, who agreed to write the episodes set in Naples and Rome, declared that this film was even more pertinent to the American viewer than *Rome Open City* "because its basic theme is the relationship between a native population and a foreign soldiery." In fact, this writer, whose work was significantly altered by Rossellini,[11] declared that for those American soldiers who had fought, drank, and loved in Italy, *Paisan* would be "an overwhelming Valentine, a mirror in which once more the whole recent past will come rushing and flooding back." In the second episode of Rossellini's film, Pasquale (Alfonsino Pasca), a Neapolitan street urchin, meets and befriends a drunk black military policeman Joe (Hylan "Dots" Johnson). Once sober, Joe realizes that Pasquale has stolen his boots. He tracks down the boy who brings him "home" to the Mergellina cave. There the American soldier views the deplorable conditions in which the boy and his neighbors live in postwar Italy. Wagstaff, in his formal analysis of the episode (*Italian Neorealist Cinema* 243–253), notes the similarity of the relationship between Joe and Pasquale with that of the protagonists of *Bicycle Thieves* (246): "As they go through Naples, the pair are very similar to Antonio and Bruno in *Ladri di biciclette,* both as a visual motif (their contrasting height and gait) and psychologically: in De Sica's film Antonio's wits are dulled by obsessive anxiety, while Bruno is alert, resourceful, and protective of his father." In fact, as Gallagher (195) reports, the episode "really took form only when Roberto [Rossellini] saw the boy and the black together exchanging lines and smiles"; this comment recalls De Sica's decision to cast Enzo Staiola as Bruno because of the contrast of his gait with that of Lamberto Maggiorani, who played his father, Antonio Ricci (Bazin 54–55). Parallels emerge between Rossellini's African American MP, Joe, and Lee's "*il gigante di cioccolata,*" Private First Class Sam Train (Omar Benson Miller) in terms of their relationships to young, orphaned Italian boys (Pasquale and Angelo respectively) as well as in their experience of the racial prejudices faced at home in the United States. Both films, I would argue, acknowledge racism in the United States while underscoring the shocking deprivations and staggering losses in Italy caused by the war.

Lee Daniels' and Spike Lee's adaptations of neorealist techniques and themes underscore the need for contextualizing film criticism in a larger, transatlantic framework instead of considering Italian and American cinematic works only in relation to their respective national film cultures. This consideration of the Italian neorealist aesthetic by African American directors forces us to gaze outward beyond the confines of national cinema to understand the use of an essentially foreign genre to comment on racism and poverty within American society. In an ironic twist, the quintessentially American problem of racism (at least in the European imagination) now threatens the social fabric of that continent as waves of immigrants enter the once homogenous societies of the past.[12] Daniels and Lee effectively project social and political critiques, just as De Sica and Rossellini did in postwar Italy. In this way, contemporary American directors demonstrate the continued vitality and relevance of Italian film for American cinema in the twenty-first century.

VI

Whither the Remake?

Remakes of foreign films represent critical junctures between two national cinemas, and indeed between two cultures. As such, they provide fertile ground for this book's investigation. Whereas the decision to make a film entails a complicated analysis of artistic merit, economic feasibility, and audience appeal for both domestic and foreign markets, the commitment to remake a film is predicated on translating the economic and artistic success of the original into an updated or entirely new cultural context. Unsurprisingly, most critics and audiences measure the success of the latest incarnation against that of the initial version. An examination of the relationship between Italy and the United States regarding the remake reveals that the transatlantic gaze peers primarily in one direction: Hollywood tends to refashion Italian films but not vice versa, with the notable exception of *È già ieri/Stork Day* (Manfredonia, 2004), starring Antonio Albanese (the *divo* in *To Rome with Love*), an Italian remake of *Groundhog Day* (Ramis, 1993), starring Bill Murray as Phil. Perhaps this phenomenon results from a perception in the United States that European films are inherently more sophisticated than American films. Or perhaps Hollywood studios cannot resist the very real economic possibilities that reframing a successful foreign film for American audiences promises. Clearly, the remake demands critical attention in order to understand the relationship between the cinemas of Italy and the United States.

Quo vadis? (Guazzoni, 1912) proved enormously successful when George Kleine brought it to the United States shortly after its release in Italy. Mervyn LeRoy's decision to remake that film in 1951 signaled a return of American production companies to Italy after a hiatus that began in 1938 and continued through the end of World War II.[1] Other notable adaptations of Italian films by American directors followed.

Mario Monicelli's Oscar-nominated film *I soliti ignoti/Big Deal on Madonna Street* (1958), itself thought to be a parody of Dassin's French heist movie *Rififi* (1955), served as the basis for two remakes:[2] *Crackers* (1984), directed by Louis Malle and set in San Francisco, and *Welcome to Collinwood* (2002), directed by Anthony and Joe Russo and set in Cleveland. These two films, which follow the original plot of a hapless group of small-time thieves who conspire to burglarize a local pawnshop, point to the pitfalls and critical considerations inherent in the remake. Vincent Canby, writing of *Crackers* in the *New York Times*, compliments veteran theatrical actor Christine Baranski and New York model Tasia Valenza for their performances, but says of the rest of the film: "In every other way, the movie is a mistake." Canby condemns the effort, saying that *Crackers* "simply proves that with the right material an intelligent director of demonstrated style and a cast of thoroughly accomplished comic actors can make as painfully witless a comedy as any knucklehead on the block." *Welcome to Collinwood* fared better with the critics. But, according to Roger Ebert, a fan of Monicelli's film featuring Vittorio Gassman, Marcello Mastroianni, and Totò, the remake, with an all-star cast including George Clooney, William Macy, and Sam Rockwell, remains haunted by the original. Ebert wonders "if the real problem is that I've seen the original. 'Welcome to Collinwood' is a wacky and eccentric heist comedy with many virtues, but it is also a remake of 'Big Deal on Madonna Street' (1958), a movie much beloved by me. Some scenes are so close to the original it's kind of uncanny." Ebert notes the invidious comparison that a remake elicits when he says that all he "could do was compare and contrast" the Russos' film to Monicelli's original. Certainly the uncanniness, or *unheimlichkeit* in German, which results when the strange becomes familiar, characterizes a remake of a foreign film. Theorists from Freud to Lacan and Kristeva have addressed the cognitive dissonance that results when something is either uncomfortably strange or familiar. Essentially negative, this phenomenon has a destabilizing effect on the viewer and thus must be considered as part of any assessment of the remake.

Dino Risi's *Profumo di Donna* (1974), an award-winning adaptation of Giovanni Arpino's novel *Il buio e il miele (The Darkness and the Honey)*, provided the material for Martin Brest's *Scent of a Woman* (1992). Plots in both films focus on the bond between

Figure 6.1. Frank Slade (Al Pacino) and Charlie Simms (Chris O'Donnell) in *Scent of a Woman*.

the older man (Fausto Consolo, played by Vittorio Gassman in the original, and Frank Slade, played by Al Pacino in the remake) and his younger assistant (Ciccio/Alessandro Momo and Chris Simms/Chris O'Donnell). Their friendship grows despite the older man's gruff demeanor, sarcasm, misanthropy, and suicidal wishes. While maintaining the general story line of a blind former army officer on a journey to oblivion in order to escape his disability (and attendant despair), the American script, written by Bo Goldman, expands the narrative to give more depth to the story of Chris Simms, the prep school scholarship student who accompanies Frank Slade. The addition of an honor code drama to the original plot emphasizes the bond between the two men in a tangible way. The relationship between Frank and Charlie deepens to a surprising degree as the older man comes to the younger man's aid during the dramatic disciplinary hearing in the final scene of Brest's film. The tense dinner scene at Frank's sister's house informs our understanding of the protagonist. Whereas Monicelli's original suggests confidence in Italian viewers' ability to grapple with ambiguity in character (and consequently in plot), Brest's version presupposes the audience's need to understand motivations behind a character's action as seen through his relationship to others.

Like Risi's original, the remake was successful with critics and at the box office. Vittorio Gassman received the award for Best Actor at Cannes and the David di Donatello in 1975; Al Pacino received an Oscar for Best Actor for his role in *Scent of a Woman* in 1993. *Profumo di Donna* also received a David di Donatello award for Dino Risi's direction in addition to two Academy Award nominations in the categories of Best Foreign Film and Best Writing, and Screenplay Adapted from Other Material in 1976. In addition to Pacino's award, Oscar nominations recognized *Scent of a Woman* in three categories: Martin Brest for Best Director and Best Picture as well as Bo Goldman for Best Writing of a Screenplay Based on Material from Another Medium.

Another highly successful, albeit controversial, Italian film from 1974, Lina Wertmüller's *Travolti da un insolito destino nell'azzurro mare d'agosto* (*Swept Away by an Unusual Destiny in the Blue Sea of August*), served as the basis for two remakes, *Overboard* (Marshall, 1987) and *Swept Away* (Ritchie, 2002). Wertmüller's dark, highly political sex comedy centers on a shipwrecked pair, Raffaella Pavone Lanzetti (Mariangelo Melato), a wealthy woman, and Gennarino Carunchio (Giancarlo Giannini), a crew member of a chartered yacht. *Swept Away* pits poor against wealthy, uneducated against educated, southern against northern Italian, and male against female in typically polemical Wertmüller fashion. Such polarizations invite the viewer to contemplate the gross inequities in the world and to sympathize with the underdog, whether in terms of wealth, politics, or gender. The exaggerated stereotypes representing Italy's political opposites—communists and social democrats (capitalists, really)—mirror the sexual tension between the couple. Recognized in Italy and abroad as a commercial success, *Swept Away* was less of a critical success, winning only one award, a David di Donatello in 1975 for best music by Piero Piccioni in the same year that Vittorio Gassman won the award for best actor in *Profumo di donna* and Mariangela Melato (the protagonist, Raffaella, in *Swept Away*) won the David di Donatello award for best actress for her work in the little-known film *La poliziotta/Policewoman* (Stefano Vanzina, 1974).

Wertmüller, who believed in producing films that would appeal to audiences and make them ponder political and social realities, was

the first woman nominated for the Academy Award for Best Director (followed in subsequent years by Jane Campion, Sofia Coppola,
and Kathryn Bigelow) for *Pasqualino Settebellezze/Seven Beauties* in
1975. At once provocative and topical, she used comedy to examine trenchant political issues. Wertmüller's choice of genre did not
enamor her to the politically progressive segments in Italian society
and filmmaking, as Marcus explains (*Italian Film* 313–314).[3] The
profoundly disturbing scenes on the deserted island (a male fantasy,
perhaps?), in which the ill-educated and brutish Gennarino abuses the
spoiled and self-absorbed Raffaella personally for the ills of her class
until she accepts the natural law of male dominance, provoked con-
sternation from critics and viewers alike.[4] Considering the emotional
and physical violence portrayed in this film, as well as the negative
critical reception, such as that of Molly Haskell ("Swept Away on a
Wave of Sexism," *Village Voice*, September 1975) and Tania Modleski
("Wertmuller's Women: Swept Away by the Usual Destiny," *Jump Cut*,

Figure 6.2. Raffaella (Mariangelo Melato) and Gennarino (Giancarlo
Giannini) in *Swept Away*.

June 1976), it is indeed surprising that Wertmüller's film was the basis for two international remakes.[5] Criticized by feminist scholars in Italy and in the United States for markedly different reasons, *Swept Away* has been remade according to the sensibilities of the American director Garry Marshall (born Garry Maschiarelli) and the British director Guy Ritchie.

In *Swept Away*, as with other films in her oeuvre, Wertmüller uses sex as a vehicle for discussing politics. Eleftheriotis (150) contends that despite the fact that her films offer no particular political solutions, but instead leave us with "a messy web of connections, contradictions and conventions," they are "intensely preoccupied with the political and ideological discourses of the time and saturated with the passion, uncertainty and anxiety of the struggles around them." Yet neither of the two remakes preserves the essential political underpinnings, especially regarding sexual inequities, which are critical to Wertmüller's original.

Marshall's *Overboard* (1987) features Goldie Hawn as Joanna, the spoiled, wealthy wife of Grant Stayton III, played by Edward Hermann, who shows his true lack of affection when she disappears, having fallen overboard while trying to retrieve her diamond ring from the back of their yacht. This improbable love story also stars Hawn's real-life partner, Kurt Russell, as the widowed carpenter Dean Proffitt. He claims Joanna as his wife and mother of his unruly boys when she suffers from amnesia after her fall. This is his recompense for the renovations to her yacht for which she refused to pay him. Marshall's film reframes Wertmüller's tale according to Hollywood's formula for romantic comedy, complete with the requisite happy ending. His film turns the originally dark tale into a romance, in which only the issue of class remains as part of the comic dynamic in putting (returning?) the uppity female in her place. Whereas Joanna tries the patience of everyone, especially the butler, Andrew (Roddy McDowall), her wealthy husband's complete disinterest makes viewers more sympathetic to her plight. Additionally, Joanna's outrageously privileged mother (Katherine Helmond) gives insight into her upbringing and allows the viewer to understand, and perhaps forgive, her spoiled ways. In sum, Joanna's appeal increases as she begins to love Dean and his family. The film's ending displays true differences between Wertmüller's dark comedy and Marshall's romantic comedy. Ultimately, Joanna, unlike Raffaella, decides to trade her loveless marriage to a wealthy man for a new life with a carpenter. Her decisive jump into the waters to swim to

Dean after being "rescued" by husband Grant underscores her transformation from the night of her accidental slip overboard. However obnoxious and entitled she appears, Joanna never intimidates to the extent that Raffaella does. Perhaps Marshall reflects a certain American democratic idealism in the character of Dean, whose surname, Proffitt, ironically suggests the fruits of capitalism to which he is not privy. He never seems as brutish (or essentially misogynistic) as Gennarino, the faithful communist, despite being a bit down on his luck when his wife dies, leaving him to raise three rambunctious boys alone. Unlike Gennarino, whose wife is quite pregnant, Dean has no spouse. The marital situations of both Joanna (whose husband is a cad) and Dean (whose wife is dead) obviate the need for any soul searching on the part of the audience. Thus Marshall's remake succeeds in pleasing American audiences by leaving politics and morality aside in this romantic comedy. It also reveals the maternal side of the heroine by portraying her as a caring surrogate mother to Dean's children. No longer is this romantic comedy solely a doomed love story between members of disparate, antagonistic social classes as in Wertmüller's film.

Ritchie's 2002 interpretation of *Swept Away* follows the original script closely. It even features Giancarlo Giannini's son Adriano as

Figure 6.3. Joanna (Goldie Hawn) and Dean (Kurt Russell) and family in *Overboard*.

Giuseppe the deckhand, who plays opposite the director's wife at the time, Madonna, in the role of Amber, a wealthy American socialite. In this film, which is essentially a vehicle for showcasing Madonna's physique, the politics are not sexy and the sex is not political. The film was an unmitigated disaster; the only prizes it won were the Razzie Awards for worst actress (Madonna), worst director (Ritchie), worst picture (Screen Gems), worst remake or sequel, and worst screen couple (Madonna and Giannini).

Other recent remakes of Italian originals have met with critical and economic failure as well. In 2006, Tony Goldwyn directed *The Last Kiss*, an American adaptation of Gabriele Muccino's *L'ultimo bacio* (2001), which stars Stefano Accorsi and Giovanna Mezzogiorno as a young, unmarried couple who are expecting a baby as they approach their thirtieth birthdays. The Italian original, an examination of the effects of impending parenthood (and fatherhood in particular) on a couple, resonated with Italian audiences. This escapist male fantasy of a father to be who has an affair with a high school girl, Francesca (Martina Stella, seventeen years old at the time), was nominated for ten David di Donatello awards in 2001 and won five in the categories of Best Director (Gabriele Muccino), Best Editing (Claudio DiMauro), Best Producer (Domenico Procacci), Best Sound (Gaetano Carito), and Best Supporting Actress (Stefania Sandrelli). Muccino's film received international acclaim at the outset, with awards at Sundance (Gabriele Muccino for World Cinema) and Newport (Claudio Santamaria for Best Actor). The American version, with a cast headed by stars Zach Braff and Casey Affleck, did not do well with critics or at the box office. Goldwyn's film received nominations from the Australian Film Institute, Satellite Awards, and Teen Choice Awards (in the chick flick category), and Rachel Bilson was nominated for a Teen Choice Award for best breakout female role. Its run in theaters was very short.

Kirk Jones's 2009 release of *Everybody's Fine*, a remake of Giuseppe Tornatore's *Stanno tutti bene* (1990), starring Marcello Mastroianni, drew equally lackluster comments from critics and similarly disappointing revenues despite a star-studded cast featuring Robert De Niro, Drew Barrymore, and Kate Beckinsale. The Italian original, which follows a Sicilian widower as he visits his children throughout the Italian peninsula, won numerous accolades, including Cannes Film Festival Prize of the Ecumenical Jury for director Giuseppe Tornatore

Figure 6.4. Matteo Scuro (Marcello Mastroianni) and daughter Tosca (Valeria Cavalli) at train station in *Stanno tutti bene*.

in 1990 in addition to Tornatore's nomination for the prestigious Palme d'Or. Ennio Morricone won a David di Donatello award for best music, and Tornatore received the silver ribbon from Italian journalists for best original story. Music was the most nominated category for the American version (Broadcast Film Critics Association Awards, Golden Globes, USA, and World Soundtrack Awards), while De Niro received a nomination from the Hollywood Film Festival for Best Actor. Writing in the *New York Times*, Holden warns the prospective viewer about the film: "The queasiness produced by this sentimental weepie builds into a wave of nausea during its interminable finale, in which a family with the usual array of problems and disappointments (I refuse to use the term "dysfunctional" anymore) reunites for Christmas, all lovey-dovey." Calling *Everybody's Fine* "false to the core" and "mechanically contrived," Holden registers his disappointment with the actors as well in this American adaptation.

The works of Federico Fellini offer perhaps the richest point of investigation on the phenomenon of the American remake of Italian originals. Fellini's *Notti di Cabiria / Nights of Cabiria* (1957), which won the Academy Award for Best Foreign Film in 1958, first became the Broadway musical *Sweet Charity* (1966), written by Neil

Figure 6.5. Frank (Robert De Niro) and Amy (Kate Beckinsale) in *Everybody's Fine*.

Simon and choreographed by Bob Fosse, and later a film by the same name directed by Bob Fosse (1969). Bosley Crowther, writing in the *New York Times*, focuses on Fellini's character development, not plot, in *Nights of Cabiria*: "Like 'La Strada' and several other of the post-war Italian neo-realistic films, this one is aimed more surely toward the development of a theme than a plot. Its interest is not so much the conflicts that occur in the life of the heroine as the deep, underlying implications of human pathos that the pattern of her life shows." Crowther correctly defines Fellini's film as an investigation into the human psyche, that includes the unattractive (and therefore depressing) elements of the feisty, yet ultimately pathetic, protagonist of the title. Cabiria (Fellini's wife, Giulietta

Figure 6.6. Cabiria
(Giulietta Masina) in
Nights of Cabiria.

Figure 6.7. Charity
Hope Valentine
(Shirley MacLaine) in
Sweet Charity.

Masina) is a prostitute, yet she owns her home, an accomplishment of which she is justifiably proud. Unlucky in love, she has negative experiences with men who steal from her at the beginning and end of the film. At one point, Cabiria finds herself in the company of a movie star, Alberto Lazzari, played by the real-life leading man Amedeo Nazzari, whose career extended over more than forty years and included roles in *Luciano Serra pilota* (1938), *Il bandito* (1946), and *Catene* (1949). Cabiria's visit to Lazzari's palatial abode occurs after he has a dramatic public fight with his girlfriend, Jessy (Maria Luisa Mangini, whose stage name was Dorian Gray). When Jessy turns up at the mansion, Cabiria must hide in the star's bathroom. Through the keyhole, she spies the couple's reconciliation in a scene that comments on the voyeuristic aspects of cinema. This perspective also offers Cabiria the critical distance to observe real romance, however melodramatic, which eludes her.

In the United States, *Nights of Cabiria* lived on as *Sweet Charity*, first as a successful Broadway musical and then as the film. The musical, written by Dorothy Fields and composed by Cy Coleman, was based on Neil Simon's adaptation of Fellini's film. Bob Fosse directed and choreographed this production, in which his wife, Gwen Verdon, starred. Through the years, there have been several revivals of the musical in London and New York. In 2005, Christina Applegate starred for a limited time in *Sweet Charity* on Broadway at the Al Hirschfield Theater. In 2012 a Hispanic version directed by Julio Agustin and starring Edlyn González as Caridad Esperanza Valentin debuted at New Haarlem Arts Theater.

At the time of its release, *Nights of Cabiria* created controversy in Italy and received tepid reviews in the United States. Fellini's decision to tell the tale of a prostitute provoked the censors; their disproval in turn affected his ability to find funding. The adaptation's title, *Sweet Charity: The Adventures of a Girl Who Wanted to Be Loved* (Fosse, 1969), reveals the American penchant for sanitizing unpleasant or socially unacceptable elements found in the Italian original. The American title lacks the cinematic references of Fellini's title. Cabiria recalls Pastrone's 1914 historical epic as well as the prostitute, played by Giulietta Masina, with whom Ivan speaks briefly in Fellini's earlier film *The White Sheik*. Fosse's title character Charity Rose Valentine (Shirley MacLaine), who plays a dance hall hostess in a Times Square locale, dilutes the sexual frankness found in Fellini's original *Nights of*

Cabiria. Sweet Charity instead presents a sort of cheery paean to hard work. Charity, like Cabiria, suffers humiliation and rejection by men at the beginning and end of the film; she, too, encounters an Italian movie star, Vittorio Vidal, played by the real-life heartthrob Ricardo Montalban. The reformulation of the film's ending from open-ended narrative pathos, in which Cabiria follows a band of young musicians into the woods after her fiancé steals her money and almost pushes her off a cliff, to the upbeat ending in which smiling Charity greets others in Central Park, signals another accommodation to American audiences and their expectations of musical comedy. Crowther's critique of Fellini's film hints at a rationale for such alterations: "But there are two weaknesses in 'Cabiria.' It has a sordid atmosphere and there is something elusive and insufficient about the character of the heroine. Her get-up is weird and illogical for the milieu in which she lives and her farcical mannerisms clash with the ugly realism of the theme." American audiences undoubtedly would reject the "sordid atmosphere" and the clash between "ugly realism" and Masina's brilliant, clownish delivery. Fellini's focus on the "nights" of Cabiria emphasizes both the darkness of human nature as well as the director's preference for the oneiric. The American version, with perky Shirley MacLaine in the lead, transpires for the most part during the light of day. The *chiaroscuro* effect of Fellini's films, which casts metaphorical and literal shadows through the alternation of the light of day and the dark of night, is seldom apparent in the American interpretation.[6]

Critics such as Addison Verrill had high hopes for this film. Writing in *BoxOffice* on February 3, 1969, he praised Fosse's directorial debut for its use of a "grab-bag of celluloid tricks" that included freeze frames, reverse action, stills, and slow motion. Despite its adult theme, the film would appeal, according to Verrill, to both female and male viewers, because no one would find it offensive. He predicted that this G-rated film, which he called a "brassy bonanza of a musical," would be a hit because it embodied "a combination that just can't be bettered on screen, and, happy news for Universal and exhibitors everywhere, most likely cannot be beat at the box office." Unfortunately for the studio, the reverse was the case: with a budget of $20 million, *Sweet Charity* returned only $4 million and almost bankrupted Universal Pictures. Vincent Canby's assessment of the film was diametrically opposed to that of Verrill. He stated that *Sweet Charity* "has been so enlarged and so inflated that it has become another maximal movie: a long, noisy and finally, dim imitation of its source material." Praising the Broadway adaptation by Neil Simon and the score by Cy Coleman and Dorothy Fields as "a triumph of theatrical style over content, a star vehicle assembled from bright objects, found and borrowed," Canby noted MacLaine's inability to register the "contradictory, funny internal anxieties" of her character: "When she is required to be pathetic, she is like an out-of-control jet fighter, yawing wildly through the sound barrier that separates pathos from bathos and oblivion." This last comment suggests Canby's understanding of and appreciation for Fellini's original premise as well as for Giulietta Masina's particular comic genius. Unsurprisingly, *Sweet Charity* won no awards.

Fellini's semiautobiographical *8½* (1963) has engendered remakes such as Woody Allen's *Stardust Memories* (1980) and, more recently, Rob Marshall's *Nine* (2009), which followed the same trajectory as *Sweet Charity*, appearing first in 1982 as a Broadway musical (written by Arthur Kopit) before becoming a film several decades later. The musical opened originally in New York, moved to London's

Figure 6.8. Guido Anselmi (Marcello Mastroianni) conducts in *8½*.

Figure 6.9. Guido Contini (Daniel Day-Lewis) and Stephanie (Kate Hudson) et al. in *Nine*.

West End, and toured the United States before finally returning to London as a revival in 2009. It won Tony Awards for Best Musical, Best Score, and Best Revival of a Musical. Maury Yeston, who wrote the music and lyrics for the Broadway production, was smitten by Fellini's autobiographical tale of an artist in crisis; in fact, he, like Fellini, saw himself in the figure of the middle-aged Guido Contini. Yeston, who was an associate professor of music theory at Yale at the time, described his identification with Fellini in an interview with Carol Lawson in *The New York Times*: "I looked at the screen and said, 'That's me.' I still believed in all the dreams and ideals of what it was to be an artist, and here was a movie about an artist—an artist in trouble. It became an obsession." But the musical's indebtedness to Fellini's film could not be mentioned anywhere as a condition of the copyright agreement (Lawson). The titles of the two works reveal a crucial difference: whereas Fellini's original computation marked his film as *8½* (because he had directed seven full-length films, two short films valued as ½ film each, as well as one film that he codirected that was also worth ½ film, in his calculation), Yeston added an additional half credit to arrive at *Nine*. He explained that the addition of music would be equivalent to a half number: "I thought, if you add music, it's like half a number more." For Yeston, " '8 ½' was always Italian opera, for it seemed to want to sing" (Lawson).

On Broadway, *Nine* was a success, just like *Sweet Charity* before it. Yet the movie met with dismal critical reception, both in the United States and in Italy, where it opened in December 2009 and January 2010, respectively. Despite substantial advertising and marketing campaigns, by March 2010 *Nine* had grossed less than $20 million after an estimated outlay of $80 million. Many critics of the film, starring Daniel Day-Lewis and highly paid actresses such as Sophia Loren, Penélope Cruz, Kate Hudson, Nicole Kidman, Judi Dench, and Fergie, were merciless. Writing in the *New York Times*, A. O. Scott summed up the American remake this way: " 'Nine' dresses up its coarseness in bogus prestige, which both kills the fun and exposes an emptiness at the project's heart—a fatal lack of inspiration. The fear of such a void is what animates the Guido character played by Marcello Mastroianni in '8 ½,' a man whose vanity, tenderness and narcissism mirrored Fellini's own, and whose anxiety at the prospect of failing as an artist and a man made him a vivid and credible hero. That psychological dimension is missing from 'Nine,' which never finds a way to communicate either the romantic ardor or the artistic passion that would make Mr. Day-Lewis's Guido interesting." Scott Foundas was particularly critical of the remake: "An assault on the senses from every conceivable direction—smash zooms, the ear-splitting eruption of something like music, the spectacle of a creature called Kate Hudson—*Nine* thrashes about in search of 'cinema' the way a child thrown into the deep end of a pool flails for a flotation device. I wondered if Marshall had ever seen a screen musical before he got the assignment. Watching *Nine*, I began to wonder if Marshall has ever seen a movie other than his own."

The Italian response to the film was equally negative. Paolo D'Agostini, writing in *La Repubblica*, noted the coincidence of the film's Italian opening with the original director's birthday in 2010:

> Il 20 gennaio Federico avrebbe compiuto novant'anni, e il 5 febbraio sarà passato mezzo secolo dall'uscita di *La dolce vita*. L'adattamento dal musical "omaggio" all'altro capolavoro felliniano *8½* poteva essere peggio di così, tuttavia non è un buon servizio alla memoria del maestro riminese. Con enorme dispendio di mezzi e star viene pedantemente

spiegato come il mondo felliniano fosse fatto di bugie e
sogni, le sue fantasie fossero popolate di preti e di sesso e
nutrite da uno sguardo infantile. Cioè, guarda un po', che
la sua vita era la sua opera. Senza riuscire neanche a sfio-
rare il senso di un'avventura, quella di *8½*, che trasformò
miracolosamente in capolavoro un vuoto di ispirazione. (On
January 20 Federico would have turned 90 and on February 5 one half-century will have passed since *La dolce vita*
premiered. Even though the musical homage to Fellini's
other masterpiece *8½* could have been worse, it still does
not do justice to the maestro from Rimini. With enormous
waste of funds and star power, this film pedantically explains
how the Fellinian world was created out of lies and dreams,
how his fantasies were populated with priests and sex and
nourished by an infantile gaze. That is, if you look at it,
how his real life was his work. Without realizing even a bit
of the spirit of *8½* that miraculously transformed lack of
inspiration into a masterpiece.)

Lietta Tornabuoni called this film a "Baracconata ridicola, che vor-
rebbe trasformare le eventuali componenti autobiografiche di *8½* di
Fellini in una biografia glamour del regista visto come nevrotico e
donnaiolo" ("Ridiculous fluff that would like to transform the autobiographical aspects of Fellini's *8½* into a glam biography of the
director as neurotic womanizer"). In his critique of the film, Zonta
pointed to the embarrassing display of poor dancing and singing in
this musical.

Perhaps the most remarkable, and I would also argue, most dis-
tinctively American, innovation in these failed remakes of Fellini's films
regards the choice of genre. With its emphasis on singing and dancing,
Bob Fosse's musical transforms Fellini's investigation of the pathos of
Nights of Cabiria into a lighthearted romp in the same way that Marshall's interpretation of *8½* turns an intensely personal consideration of
the artist's relationship to his work into a string of highly choreographed
song and dance routines. The shift in genre, from psychological drama
to musical, the quintessentially American genre, complicates the adaptation's relationship to the original. Music was certainly critical to Fellini's
films, and the director's collaboration with Nino Rota helped define
the oneiric world that he sought to create. Yet despite the emphasis on

spectacle and its production in his works, the drama of understanding oneself remains the central question for Fellini.

The musical film, which begins with the advent of sound in the 1930s, draws many elements from musical theater. This genre proved a successful vehicle for films such as *Top Hat*, the 1935 musical starring Fred Astaire and Ginger Rogers (with lyrics by Irving Berlin), which features prominently in Woody Allen's *The Purple Rose of Cairo*. The musical continued to have success until the late 1960s and early 1970s, when Hollywood produced a series of flops including *Camelot*, *Finian's Rainbow*, *Hello Dolly!*, *Man of La Mancha*, and *Mame*. Several of these financially disastrous productions, including *Sweet Charity*, threatened the economic stability of the studios.[7] The musical, as Feuer (*Hollywood Musical* 84) points out, contains marked differences between speech and song, dreaming and waking, walking and dancing. Synthesis, achieved by the reconciliation of these differences, is its goal. As a genre, the musical film creates entirely different expectations than one finds in Fellini's open-ended and unresolved narratives. Although *Sweet Charity* does not end in marriage, for Oscar leaves Charity at the Marriage Bureau, the message is still quite optimistic, as Charity smiles and greets others in the park after the hippies shower her with love and flowers. The morning after Oscar abandons her, Charity "lived hopefully ever after," according to the inter-title that allows the viewer to imagine that one day "just" might replace "almost" married on her honeymoon suitcase. In fact, Fosse filmed an alternate ending, now available as extra material on the DVD, for fear that the studios would demand a definitively happy ending. In the substitute version, Oscar encounters Charity when he goes for a walk in Central Park after the breakup. He runs to save her from what he thinks is a suicide attempt. When he trips and falls into the water, she tries to save him even though she cannot swim. Oscar saves Charity and then proposes again.

The musical film serves as a powerful reminder of the image-making possibility of Hollywood, as well as of the optimism that characterizes much of American culture. In terms of genre, the musical underscores a profound difference between Hollywood and Italy in the postwar period. There are very few musical films in Italy. The director Roberta Torre has embraced the musical in order to parody the social conventions of the South with *Tano da morire/To Die for Tano* (1997) and *Sud side stori/South Side Story* (1999). O'Healy (47–49) reports that Torre's first musical, which lampooned Mafia culture, proved a tremendous success with Italian audiences despite its critical view of Sicilians and their society.[8] Marcus indicates the paradoxical effectiveness of the film's genre in pursuit of a political message when she says that "by reveling in the artifice of musical comedy, Torre's film promotes and renews the agenda of Italy's most hallowed realist tradition—that of heightening public understanding of social problems in order to lead toward intervention" (*After Fellini* 234). Marcus identifies the *sceneggiata*, the Neapolitan musical drama, as the basis for this type of film, which, on account of its roots in southern culture, is an appropriate vehicle for the critique of organized crime (*After Fellini* 244–245). Originally performed in theaters, the *sceneggiata*, a narrative staging of songs, was adapted for films following the First World War (Bruno 168). The filmic interpretation of this genre re-emerged in the 1970s in the regional cinema of the south and of Naples in particular.[9]

Nanni Moretti offers insight into reading the contemporary Italian reception of musicals in his highly autobiographical film *Caro diario/Dear Diary* (1993). In this film he plays himself instead of

Figure 6.10. Nanni Moretti plays himself in *Dear Diary*.

his cinematic alter ego, Michele Apicella, as in previous films. In the aptly titled first chapter of his diary, "In Vespa," Moretti cruises through Roman neighborhoods on his motor scooter. In order to see inside a Roman penthouse, Nanni pretends to be looking for a location to shoot a film, which he describes for the owner as "la storia di un pasticcere trotskista nell'Italia degli anni 50—un film musicale, un musical" ("the story of a Trotskyite pastry chef in 1950s Italy—a musical film"). Here, Moretti, whose role as both director and protagonist compounds his critique, comments on the ridiculous notion of an Italian musical. The assumption that the audience will also find the musical comical presupposes a general Italian disregard for this genre. Yet, ultimately and ironically, Moretti concludes his subsequent film *Aprile/April* (1998) with scenes from the very film for which he pretended to scout locations in *Dear Diary*.[10] *April*, a work that addresses both Moretti's impending fatherhood and the national elections with which he is consumed, extends the director's autobiographical inquiry that was established in *Dear Diary*. At the end of *April*, Moretti succeeds in completing his musical in which young women sport pastel costumes that match the pastries they create while dancing with male chefs in colorful toques. This whimsical confection allows the viewer to appreciate the absurdity of the musical genre for the Italian imagination.

Moretti's apparent send-up of the über-American genre of the musical is inscribed in a larger contemplation of the intersection of American and Italian cinemas in *Dear Diary*. The director criticizes journalists whose positive reviews of *Henry: Portrait of a Serial Killer* (McNaughton, 1986), a low-budget splatter film based on the life of serial killer Henry Lee Lucas, ultimately catapulted it to the Chicago and Telluride film festivals. Moretti's determination to dance like Jennifer Beals (who makes a cameo appearance with then husband Alexandre Rockwell in *Dear Diary*) signals an appreciation of, or an obsession with, the star of the American blockbuster film *Flashdance* (1983). When Nanni's traveling companion, Gerardo (Renato Carpentieri), asks American tourists about the soap opera *The Bold and the Beautiful*, which premiered on CBS in 1987 and is still running today, the viewer understands that this TV-hating, Hans Magnus Enzensberger-quoting intellectual has become a devoted fan. Gerardo's explanation that the Americans are ahead of the Italians (in terms of episodes) suggests a more trenchant observation about the relationship between the two media cultures. A conversation on Stromboli in the second chapter, "Isole" ("Islands"), between Moretti and American tourists hints at another connection between the two countries. Near the crater of the iconic volcano on that Aeolian island, tourists answer Gerardo's questions about *The Bold and the Beautiful* that Nanni reads in English. Their report that Macy's marriage is over because of a love affair with her tennis instructor recalls the scandal behind the scenes of Rossellini's *Stromboli, terra di Dio/Stromboli* (1950). Ingrid Bergman, who played Karin, the desperate foreign wife of an island native, deserted her husband Petter Lindstrom and children in California when she began a shocking affair with Rossellini while filming on the island.[11] Thus Moretti's *Dear Diary*, a cinematic palimpsest, subtly reveals many of Italy's associations with Hollywood while critiquing the characteristics of the quintessential American musical with its illusion of spontaneity and effortlessness.

Throughout the history of cinema, Italian film has influenced American cinema to varying degrees. This investigation demonstrates that the success of American adaptations of Italian cinema depends in large part on genre. As this chapter has shown, transnational adaptations of certain genres, such as comedy, have succeeded while others, such as the musical, have not. The challenge of adapting Italian material to the American context seems irresistible to Hollywood. No doubt the allure of Italian cinema will continue to captivate and inspire remakes by American directors in the future, just as it has in the past.

VII

Conclusion

"I've always been influenced by the spaghetti western. I used to describe 'Pulp Fiction' as a rock n' roll spaghetti western with the surf music standing in for Ennio Morricone. I don't know if 'Django' is a western proper. It's a southern. I'm playing western stories in the genre, but with a southern backdrop."

—Quentin Tarantino in an interview with Charles McGrath

This volume has analyzed the dialogue that exists between directors in Italy and those in the United States through deliberate pairings of films. It has focused on the exchange of ideas, techniques, and narratives that has resulted in modifications, both subtle and obvious, to various genres. As *Django Unchained* (Tarantino, 2012) demonstrates, this process is dynamic. Tarantino's latest film allows us to follow the trajectory of the Western genre as it mutates from the classical, American interpretation through the radical Italian version of the 1960s before becoming the postmodern "southern" that addresses the politically charged issue of slavery. We have seen how Leone's spaghetti Western *Once Upon a Time in the West* employs the Western genre in order to critique accepted notions of progress. As Fischer (197–198) points out, when American filmmakers adapted some of the conventions of the spaghetti Western, they tended to downplay the political elements while increasing the volume and intensity of violence. Thus, a subset of the Western that employs extreme (and seemingly unwarranted, in some cases) violence tends to ignore one of its basic tenets, namely the critique of American expansionism, hegemony, colonial power, and unwarranted brutality to native cultures. When elements of the spaghetti Western return to American cinema, for example, in Tarantino's *Kill Bill* saga (2003, 2004), what remains is the violence, which the director gleefully appropriates. Fischer (200) criticizes Tarantino, as well as Rodriguez, his codirector in *Grindhouse* (2007), for having stripped the spaghetti Western of meaning, saying: "In an environment so obsessed with violence of a purely cinematic nature, discourses pertaining to specific disputes within the 1960s Italian New Left become somewhat obscured." Yet clearly *Django Unchained*, with its focus on slavery in the pre–Civil War South, demonstrates Tarantino's insistence on the political concerns characteristic of the spaghetti Western.

Tarantino's decision to address slavery in *Django Unchained* has elicited varied critical reactions. The *New York Times* critic A. O. Scott ("The Black, the White") compares Tarantino's latest film with Spielberg's classic Hollywood production *Lincoln* (2012), which focuses on personalities and politicking in a visually and emotionally rich treatment of slavery: "You could almost imagine the two films, or at least their heroes, figuring in the kind of good-natured, racial-stereotype humor that used to be a staple of stand-up comedy (and was memorably parodied on 'The Simpsons'): 'white guys abolish slavery like this' (pass constitutional amendment); 'but black guys, they abolish slavery like this' (blow up plantation)." Calling *Django Unchained* "digressive, jokey, giddily brutal and ferociously profane," Scott views this film, which combines B-movie genres such as martial arts movies, Blaxploitation films, and spaghetti Westerns, as a contribution to the discussion on slavery and racism in the United States. George, on the other hand, reads the student–teacher relationship between Django and Dr. Shultz as potentially problematic, for it suggests black submission to white authority. Tarantino's treatment of the title character indeed recalls earlier black cowboys, such as Herb Jeffries in *Harlem on the Prairie* (Newfield, 1937), Woody Strode in *Sergeant Rutledge* (John Ford, 1960), Bill Cosby in *Man and Boy* (Swackhamer, 1971), Sidney Poitier and Harry Belafonte in *Buck and the Preacher* (Poitier, 1972), Cleavon Little in *Blazing Saddles* (Brooks, 1974), and Morgan Freeman in *Unforgiven* (Eastwood, 1992).[1] Black cowboys have had a presence in American military since the Civil War as Buffalo Soldiers. Spike Lee, who memorializes twentieth-century Buffalo Soldiers in *Miracle at St. Anna*, registered his vehement disapproval of Tarantino's film when he tweeted shortly after the film's release: "American Slavery Was Not A Sergio Leone Spaghetti Western.

It Was A Holocaust. My Ancestors Are Slaves. Stolen From Africa. I Will Honor Them." Yet *Django Unchained* makes another, more subtle political statement when Django's captors decide that work at the LeQuint Dickey Mining Company will be more severe punishment than death by castration. The suggestion that backbreaking (slavelike) work in the mines will "neuter" the potent black slave perhaps serves as a sly critique of the indignities associated with such work. Thus, with *Django Unchained* Tarantino appears to embrace not simply the searing violence of the spaghetti Western, but its ideological motivations as well.

This study has demonstrated that the inclusion or exclusion of political and ethical concerns allows the viewer to understand the differences between Italian originals and their subsequent American adaptations. The confluence of genre and political message remains consistent across the Atlantic, I argue, in the case of African American directors' embrace of the neorealist sensibility. Lee's treatment of racism suffered by African Americans during the Second World War, a conflict that essentially pitted Italy and the United States against one another, as well as Daniels' exposé of poverty and abuse in contemporary society, prove the sustained power of neorealism to critique injustices across cultures and time periods. These directors' reappropriation of the neorealist sensibility preserves the ideological essence that characterized that genre in postwar Italy.

Other genres examined in this book reveal ideology as a basis for comparison of Italian and American films. For example, Marshall's adaptation of Wertmüller's dark comedy *Swept Away* transforms black comedy into romantic comedy, social satire into love story in which the politics of sex disappear, with only the notion of class consciousness remaining. In the end, everything turns out fine in *Overboard*, while the opposite occurs in Wertmüller's film. Conversely, De Palma reinvents Antonioni's art film *Blow-Up* by emphasizing political machinations so that his audience might understand the motivations for the crimes in *Blow Out*. In *Blow-Up*, the reason behind the murder is inconsequential, for Thomas as well as for the viewer. Hence De Palma's inclusion of politics as a raison d'être reveals how an American context and aesthetic can transform an art film such as *Blow-Up* into a different genre, that of the detective thriller, in *Blow Out*.

Before one concludes that Americans do not or cannot appreciate art films, it is important to note the recent debut of several particularly challenging films that were embraced by viewers in the United States. Writing in the *New York Times*, critics A. O. Scott and Manohla Dargis discuss the narratives of films released in the autumn 2012, such as *Cloud Atlas* (Andy and Lana Wachowski, Tom Tykwer) and *The Master* (Paul Thomas Anderson), in which "filmmakers are pushing hard against, and sometimes dispensing with, storytelling conventions, and audiences seem willing to follow them" (1). Dargis explains that each year she and fellow critic Scott examine "experimental" films that "dispatch with either whole or part of the mainstream storytelling playbook" (1). Absent well-defined acts or motivated characters, the films appear to "drift along rather than shift into drive; in other words, they look a lot or a little like art films" (1). Fellow critic Scott says of reactions to *The Master:* "The divide seems to be not between people who 'get it' and those who don't, but rather between those who are frustrated by not getting it and those (like me) who enjoyed it even though we didn't get it" ("When Do We" 14). Scott could be speaking of Antonioni's *Blow-Up* when he says that these films "venture into the realm of the confounding" and that *The Master*, for example, "unfolds with what seems to be a total disregard for the audience's expectations. The movie does not explain its characters, or offer any of them up for us to like or identify with. Instead of building to a dramatic climax it seems to taper off, to let go of the strange emotional intensity that had built up over more than two hours" (14).

New relationships between directors and their audiences have developed in recent years, and, as Dargis points out, that change has profoundly affected filmmaking. The luxury of multiple viewings of one film—initially on videotape and now on DVD or on demand—has permitted directors to engage in more sustained interactions with their audiences than ever before. Thomas Elsaesser has deemed films such as Christopher Nolan's *Memento* (2000) and *Inception* (2010) "mind-game films"; these films typically are predicated on the idea that the audience will see a film multiple times in order to discover hidden clues. In this way, fans become knowledgeable film critics. Yet perhaps the most important insight from Scott's and Dargis's assessment for this investigation is their contention that films are in dialogue with one another across cultures and time periods. Dargis (14) focuses on the common thread in the experimental films: "Yet what all these new movies share—and what seems another component of the 'mind-game film'—is that they are made by directors who have a self-aware relationship with film history and their status as auteurs. Being an auteur is essential to their identity (and, blech, brand) and to their relationship with their audiences, that have been taught to recognize that even the latest Batman movie carries a director's credit, his stylistic signature and meanings that the dedicated can take to with pickaxes and endless blog postings." Thus the departure from the old Hollywood system, which sought to erase any authorial vestiges in order to render the director invisible, signals new possibilities for American cinephiles to appreciate the continuing discourse between Italian and American auteurs.

The American (Corbijn, 2010) exemplifies the complexities of precisely this kind of cross-cultural cinematic exchange. The Dutch director explicitly declares Leone's place in cinematic history when George Clooney, in the title role, sits in a bar in the tiny village of Castel del Monte in the Apennine Mountains. As Once Upon a Time in the West (1968) plays on the television in the background, the bartender looks at the screen, then back at his American customer, and says: "Sergio Leone. Italiano." The emphasis on the adjective italiano underscores the difference between the americano of the film's title (and nationality of its lead actor) and the famous director of spaghetti Westerns whose works influenced filmmakers in the United States. Corbijn draws explicit parallels in this scene between Jack/Edward (nicknamed "Mr. Butterfly"), who has embarked on building a gun for his last hired assassination, and Frank (Henry Fonda), Leone's cruel antihero and child killer. In the scene featured from Once Upon a Time in the West on the bar television, Frank and his men arrive at the Sweetwater ranch intent on murdering the entire McBain family. They succeed in carrying out the orders from railroad baron Morton who sees the land's water as critical for his steam engines. Young Timmy, the lone survivor of the ambush, runs out of the house after the carnage that has killed his father, sister, and older brother. Tragically for the boy, one of Frank's men addresses him by name when asking about what they plan to do about the child. With his identity now revealed, Frank sees no choice but to pull the trigger on the youngest McBain. This clip in The American, like the scene in the original, ends with a gunshot. In Leone's film that sound merges with the locomotive's whistle, indicating Leone's critique of progress, while in Corbijn's film the gunshot coincides with the slamming of

Figure 7.1. *Once Upon a Time in the West* poster.

the door as Clooney's character, a hit man intent on completing his last assignment, exits the bar. This neat parallel unites the two assassins, Frank (Fonda) and Jack/Edward (Clooney).

This film within the film allows the viewer to read *The American* in the context of the Western, which Corbijn claims to have followed according to the film's Web site: "I haven't seen that many movies in my life, but Westerns have long made an impression on me, starting with—in childhood—*Rawhide* (the 1960s TV series starring Clint Eastwood). The look, the stories, the morality of movie Westerns always attracted me. Although *The American* is not actually a Western, it is structured in that genre; a stranger comes to a small town and connects with a couple of people in it, but his past catches up with him—and there is a shootout." Noting that in *The American*, as in Westerns, "there is a man who has lived by the gun, and the violence that he's lived by threatens to infect the peace that he's tried to find in a place that he thinks he could live in," the film's producer Anne Carey draws similar comparisons between this film and the quintessential American genre in the production notes on the film's Web site. And *Slate* critic Dana Stevens reads this film as "a latter-day, Zen spaghetti Western, with Clooney as the Man With No Name." Clearly, Corbijn's *The American* underscores the continuing dialogue on genre between directors that the aforementioned clip from Leone's spaghetti Western highlights.

Although Cobijn's film retains its American nature in the title, lead actor, and funding and distribution, *The American* is essentially an international production. It features a Dutch director, an Italian setting in the Abruzzo region (with the exception of the brief and terrifying first scene on a frozen lake in Sweden), a mainly European cast, and British screenplay (by Rowan Joffe), based on *A Very Private Gentleman* by British novelist Martin Booth. This type of international artistic and financial collaboration gives the film a hybrid nature. The pace of *The American* diverges from mainstream Hollywood fare, as critics have noted. Michael Atkinson, in *Sight and Sound*, compares this psychological thriller positively to two British spy movies from 1965, noting the film's subtlety:

> I don't think I've ever seen a Hollywood movie as enraptured with silence. Director Anton Corbijn, vet only of *Control* and years of music videos, is completely with the Clooney programme, and in a day and age when American films are routinely packed like jack-in-the-boxes with digital cuts and overstated soundtrack madness, he's made a movie that may be only as pensive and withholding as Clooney et al remember the New Wave movies being. In other words, *The American* could make even *The Ipcress File* and *The Spy Who Came in from the Cold* look positively melodramatic by comparison.

As Atkinson notes, this film embodies European sensibilities that surprisingly enthralled American audiences despite its slow pace and retro feel evocative of the 1970s. *The American*'s success is even more impressive considering the timing of its debut. James Berardinelli points out that the film was released shortly before Labor Day weekend, which is not the most propitious time for a premiere. He wonders if perhaps Focus Features believed that *The American* would not appeal to mainstream audiences in the United States. Viewers and critics alike responded positively to the film. Berardinelli notes the film's sophistication: "Despite the presence of a major movie star in the cast (likely the reason it's being released in multiplexes), the material is suited to specialty audiences—those whose tastes gravitate toward the cerebral work of Le Carre and Deighton rather than the visceral thrills of Fleming and Ludlum. Anyone who understands what *The American* offers should come away pleased with the final product." The fact that this film succeeded in American markets suggests the viability of such international productions that embody nuanced artistic traditions typical of foreign films.

The clip from this self-consciously international production illustrates the continuing impact of Italian cinema on American filmmaking as it calls attention to Leone's legacy.[2] As this investigation has revealed, there has been a long tradition of international collaboration and exchange in filmmaking across the Atlantic. As cinema becomes more global, the notion of national cinemas becomes more complicated and ambiguous. In the future, "national" categories of cinema may disappear, as Elsaesser and others suggest. Yet I contend that we will continue to discern the influence of directors from a particular country, who represent developed aesthetics such as those found in Italian cinema. The identification of historical roots of international exchange, collaboration, and competition in the film industry will continue to inform our study, and increase our appreciation, of cinema in the future.

The Transatlantic Gaze has demonstrated the enduring impact of a variety of genres of Italian film on American directors. Despite the changes that lie ahead in filmmaking, there is good reason to believe that American directors will continue to gaze across the Atlantic for inspiration from the rich tradition and developed aesthetics found in Italian cinema in the next one hundred years.

Notes

Chapter I

1. All translations are mine unless otherwise noted.

2. According to Caranti (166), "*Cabiria* si distingue invece nel mondo, poiché, a differenza di molti altri film, viene distribuito in ogni continente." "*Cabiria* distinguishes itself in the world, because, unlike many other films, it was distributed on every continent."

3. Paolo and Vittorio Taviani include a fictional depiction of this visit in their film *Good Morning, Babylon* (1987).

4. Kleine also imported films as well for the Italian émigré community. The popularity of Italian cinema among Italian Americans is documented in Kleine's correspondence, now in the Library of Congress. He negotiated eagerly and effectively on behalf of the Hollywood studios to ensure that Italian films were distributed in this country, and then later that American films enjoyed wide distribution in Italy. For a discussion of early Italian cinema in America, see Bertellini, who makes an eloquent case for the transatlantic trade of the picturesque from Italy to America in the chapter titled "The Picturesque Italian South as International Commodity," 47–93. See also Abel.

5. See "Mussolini's Roach," as well as Ricci (66) and Ward (100).

6. For a discussion of this phenomenon, see Brunetta ("The Long March"). Jarratt (40–43) delineates the four "planks" of fascist intervention in the film industry and chronicles the establishment of ENAIPE (Ente Nazionale Importazione Pellicole Estere—National Board for the Purchase and Importation of Foreign Films), the complete state monopoly for the purchase of foreign films by distributors.

7. See Forgacs and Gundle (124–145) for a discussion of the phenomenon.

8. For the use of Cinecittà as refugee camp, see Steimatsky.

Chapter II

1. Allen collaborated with cinematographer Darius Khondji on this magnificent rendering of the Eternal City (Sciolino).

2. According to the *Online Etymology Dictionary*, the term, which first appeared in 1922, derives from the French in the masculine form of *gigole*, meaning "tall, thin woman; dancing girl; prostitute," or perhaps from verb *gigoter*, "to move the shanks, hop," from *gigue*, "shank," also "fiddle," of Germanic origin. This may be the same word that was borrowed earlier in mid–fourteenth-century Middle English as *giglot*, meaning "lewd, wanton girl," which was later applied to men sometime in the 1520s with the meaning of "villainous man." The Middle English term *gigletry* meant "lasciviousness" in the late fourteenth century.

3. Leider (371–375) describes Valentino's reaction to the editorial. The actor placed an open letter in the *Herald Examiner* addressing the anonymous author of the piece, who had attacked "me, my race, and my father's name. You slur my Italian ancestry; you cast ridicule upon my Italian name; you cast doubt upon my manhood." Valentino then challenged the author, who never responded, to a boxing match.

4. Ellenberger chronicles the struggle over Valentino's corpse as well as the cross-country train journey from New York to its final resting place in Hollywood Cemetery (70–101).

5. According to Sordi (19), the film

urtò la suscettibilità di tutti gli editori di fotoromanzi, incluso Rizzoli, che se la presero. Alla Mostra di Venezia del 1952 andò molto male, proteste, fischi, strilli: alla critica di costume piuttosto che al film, credo, e credo che la gazzarra fosse organizzata dagli amici del fotoromanzo. (struck a sensitive chord with all the publishers of *fotoromanzi*, including Rizzoli, which got all worked up. At the Venice Exhibition of 1952 the film did poorly; there were protests, booing, yelling, more critique of values than of the film. I think that the protest was organized by the friends of the *fotoromanzo*.)

6. Del Buono 6–7; see also Bravo and Anelli et al. regarding the *fotoromanzo*.

7. The author Italo Calvino remembered going to the movies nearly every day of his childhood in 1930s Italy (Sorlin 72).

8. "Ma è con il ritiro delle *majors* americane dal mercato italiano che la commedia hollywoodiana, sparendo dagli schermi, venne maggiormente imitiata, nonostante i proposti nazionalistici del regime fascista." ("However

it was with the exit of the American major studios from the Italian market that Hollywood-style cinema, which had disappeared from the theaters, was imitated to a great degree despite the nationalist edicts of the fascist regime") (Casadio 21).

9. Fellini rendered his own version of this iconic Hollywood dancing couple in *Ginger and Fred* (1986), starring Giulietta Masina and Marcello Mastroianni as the retired stars whose reunion on a variety show reveals the vicissitudes of television and the aging process.

10. In an interview at Woolsey Hall on the Yale campus in 2011, Morgan Freeman, the actor who plays Charlie in *Nurse Betty*, expressed his love for the movies in an example of life imitating art: "I went to the movies everyday. Movies, movies, movies. Everyone I liked was in the movies."

Chapter III

1. Cuccu notes that neither the photographer nor the woman is named, but that they are called Thomas and Jane respectively in many reviews. According to him, these names were probably taken from publicity materials distributed at the time of the film's opening (17n). In the original screenplay in Italian, the protagonist is called "Il fotografo," but in the English translation, he is referred to initially as the young man, photographer, and then Thomas. I refer to the protagonists as Thomas and Jane in this chapter.

2. While the majority of reviews were positive, several major critics, including Judith Crist of *New York Herald Tribune* and Pauline Kael of *The New Yorker* separated themselves from the popular stir created by the film's arrival in the United States. Crist called the film a "cheat," and Kael, in her review for *The New Republic* (reprinted in *For Keeps: 30 Years at the Movies*), criticized Antonioni, whom she felt "simply exploits the ready-made symbolic meanings people attach to certain details and leaves us in a profound mess. (The middlebrow moralists think it's profound and the hippies enjoy the mess)." She also stated, "Antonioni, like his fashion-photographer hero, is more interested in getting pretty pictures than in what they mean. But for reasons I can't quite fathom, what is taken to be shallow in his hero is taken to be profound in him" (110–111).

3. The expression "Peeping Tom" originates from the legend of Lady Godiva; it refers to a man named Tom who watched her ride and was struck blind or dead.

4. In a contentious interview with Marcia Pally in 1984, De Palma declares that he likes women, although he finds sex terrifying. The anti-porn lobby tends to discount his appreciation of women, but De Palma insists upon his work as a VISUAL STYLIST (his capitalization). MacKinnon

outlines the issues that have arisen in De Palma's oeuvre and the feminist reaction to his films that equates his works (notably *Dressed to Kill, Body Double,* and also *Carrie*) with pornography.

5. Mulvey later reconsidered her views on this matter in subsequent writings on women and film.

6. There was a case of life imitating art in the production of *Blow Out*: the final chase scene at the end of the film was stolen from the production truck, forcing De Palma to shoot that scene again. For De Palma, this accident resonated with the film itself: "It wasn't planned, it was a ridiculous event that just occurred. It's like *Blow Out*—it was a very haphazard accident" (Amata 81).

7. Freccero emphasizes the literary notion of the film by noting the importance of the book that Thomas is compiling. He reads this film as an attempt at autobiography.

8. From an interview titled "La storia del cinema la fanno i film" in *Parla il cinema italiano* and now collected in *Architecture of Vision* 209.

9. Cortázar's title, a Spanish commonplace that means a close call, refers to a narrow escape from Satan's fangs. In this way, the title speaks to Thomas's close encounter with evil and vindication of truth through image making and offers a complex commentary on salvation in a modern context. See Bittini.

10. Comparing this film with *Blow-Up*, Bliss (n. 116) says that the message is clear: "we can never hope to possess the 'total truth' about any situation through a calculated, scientific evaluation of supposedly objective evidence. Only human empathy can aid us in approaching 'the facts.'"

11. For a discussion of this phenomenon in Antonioni's later film *Zabriskie Point* (1970), see Mazzotta.

12. Rifkin (20) mentions the term when he identifies the camera as barrier, stating that "the distance that Thomas, the photographer, assumes in order to 'get his shots' renders him not only a doubting Thomas, but also a Peeping Tom." Harrison (44) deemed *Blow-Up* "the worst kind of intellectual sentimentality" and critiqued Thomas's behavior at the end, saying of his return of the imaginary tennis ball: "He does so, and the Thomas once so sure he could interpret what was real, confesses himself a doubting Thomas, a humble, ignorant Thomas." Eberwein (266) quotes the critic Goldstein in order to prove his Oedipal reading of this figure by drawing parallels between Thomas and the supposed murderer: "A glimpse of the possible murderer through the restaurant window tells us he is young and fair-haired, a physical double for Thomas . . ." While I disagree with this psychoanalytical approach to the film, I find the idea of Thomas's double supportive of the biblical reading in that Thomas was called Didymus because he was a twin.

13. In "Antonioni's Doubting Thomas: Resurrection and Self-Discovery in *Blow-Up*," I read *Blow-Up* as a conversion narrative, drawing parallels between Thomas the apostle and Thomas the photographer, both of whom realize the limits of vision in their search for truth.

Chapter IV

1. For a discussion of the idea of the West, see Kitses (64). Cawelti (*Six-Gun* 102) notes that progress was not always a collective improvement in American terms, either.

2. For a full discussion of the terminology, see Brunetta (*Storia* 777) and Miccichè (110).

3. Miccichè (115) notes the presence of "bambini trucidati, animali sventrati, uomini accecati, sicari bruciati a fuoco lento nemici scalpati vivi dettagli anatomici sparsi nelle strade polverose e nei saloon" ("slaughtered children, gutted animals, blinded men, killers boiled alive, scalped enemies, various bits of anatomy on the dusty roads and in the saloons").

4. In his critique of this film, Hamill ("Once" 22) identifies American involvement in Vietnam as one of the extenuating circumstances contributing to the lack of popularity of *Once Upon a Time in the West* in the United States because, in 1969, "all notions of good and bad, or redemption through violence, were being widely questioned."

5. Leone's pseudonym, Bob Robertson, points to the interplay of American and Italian cinema. It also indicates his admiration for his father, whose nom de plume was Roberto Roberti, or Bob Roberts in English. Despite the fact that Vincenzo Leone was a less popular director of sentimental, dialect comedies (Frayling 65), as a young boy Sergio believed that his father had invented cinema, according to Hamill ("Leone" 23).

6. French (58) notes how casting offers clues to reading the film:

> Taken along with familiar plots and recurrent situations, these well-known, and increasingly well-worn faces serve to give the Western its quality of dejà vu and reinforce the sense of ritual. The physical presence and established properties of these actors have become part of the genre's iconography, to be accepted literally or to be worked into new patterns or mined for fresh meanings. Alone or in conflict with each other they determine the tone of a picture, and most directors are intuitively aware of the way an actor's image and attributes can be manipulated and within what limits.

7. Frayling (59–61) discusses how many of the spaghetti Westerns exhibit "amoral familism," a term coined by Edward Banfield in *The Moral Basis of a Backward Society*, which analyzed the root causes of abject poverty in southern Italy in the 1950s. Citing Barzini's *The Italians*, Frayling compares the growth of families of bandits in Westerns with that of the Mafia in southern Italy.

8. Hill (206) is the exception; while rejecting the notion that Leone has created a feminist character, she considers the problem of Jill's classification outside the traditional binary division of the Western.

9. Pezzotta (133) notes that Corbucci breaks the Hollywood mold in terms of female representation with Maria in *Django*. He says: "Fantasmi maschilisti a parte, un altro innovativo del film di Corbucci si trova nel rilievo dato alla componente femminile. Il personaggio di Maria ha un'intraprendenza che appare insolita, se si accetta la tesi di un western italiano dove le donne hanno solo ruoli secondari." ("Macho fantasies aside, another innovation in Corbucci's film is found in the prominence given to female roles. The character of Maria appears groundbreaking in terms of initiative if one accepts the premise that women in spaghetti Westerns have only secondary roles").

10. Tarantino named his 2007 film, directed with Robert Rodriguez, *Grindhouse*. This double feature of *Planet Terra* (Rodriguez) and *Death Proof* (Tarantino) combines action, horror, and exploitation and includes several fake trailers.

11. This proposition also recalls the traditional Mediterranean legal solution to rape by which marriage to the victim exonerates the rapist of his crime. For a discussion of sexual offenses and their consequences in the Roman world, see Gardner (117–136).

12. In his structural study of the Western, Wright (29–123) identifies four major plot lines: classical, vengeance variation, transition theme, and professional. See also Jameson's critique of Wright.

13. Despite this claim, Leone went on to direct another Western *Giù la testa/Duck, You Sucker* (1971). The studios had insisted that he complete *Once Upon a Time in the West* before he could start filming *Once Upon a Time in America* (1984), the ambitious three-hour saga, set in the Lower East Side, that focuses on friendship, Prohibition, and the Jewish mob.

Chapter V

1. Ruberto and Wilson's edited volume *Italian Neo-Realism and Global Cinema* examines the extensive influence of this genre on filmmaking throughout the world. See also Giovacchini and Sklar.

2. See also Pontuale (121) on this topic.

3. The commonly used English title, *Bicycle Thief,* calls attention to problems of translation; this film should be called *Bicycle Thieves* in order to be true to both the narrative and title of the Italian original.

4. In Moravia's novel, Rosetta is eighteen years old, but the youthful Sophia Loren, who was cast at the insistence of her husband, producer Carlo Ponti, needed a younger child in order for the story to make sense. Marcus (*Filmmaking by the Book*, 67–90) provides a detailed description of the adaptation of this novel to the screen. In his autobiography, Zeffirelli (216–218) explains how Ponti launched Loren's career with this film once Antonioni decided not to direct it.

5. See R. Atkinson (557–558) for a description of post armistice events and Bimberg for a discussion of the Goumier troops. For a treatment of the region of Ciociaria, see Vitti and Faustini.

6. We note parallels between this scene and Visconti's *Bellissima* (1951). In an interview with Cardullo (*After Neorealism* 22), Visconti noted the flaw in neorealism that seemed to exclude fantasy in that film:

> The big mistake of neorealism, to my way of thinking, was its unrelenting and sometimes dour concentration on social reality. What neorealism needed, and got in a film like De Sica's *Miracle in Milan* [1951] and even Pietro Germi's *The Road to Hope* [1950], was a "dangerous" mixture of reality and romanticism. I hope that I supplied this in *Bellissima*, as well. After all, these are poor people, the characters in this film, and to enable her family to escape from poverty, the mother turns to the dream-world or fantasy-factory of the popular cinema. Now that's a romantic notion! Yet, at the same time, the mother returns to sobering reality at the conclusion of the picture, and she accepts it—accepts that the illusionary world of show business is a kind of bad drug to which her own impoverished condition is far more acceptable, as long as it is ameliorated by the love of one's family. This is another romantic notion, of course, but it's firmly grounded in social reality. So we are back in the world of neorealism at the end, with a slight yet elevating twist. And thus I tried to have it "both ways" in this film.

7. Landy's reading of the relationship between mother and daughter in *Two Women* offers another possible connection between the victims of rape and their abusive mothers. She points out that in De Sica's film "Cesira still cannot accept the violation of her daughter and displaces her rage at the rape and its effects by becoming abusive toward Rosetta" (292).

8. With a budget of $58 million, the film made approximately $50 million in the first four months, according to the Internet Movie Database statistics.

9. On July 30, 1944, the first black combat infantry team landed in Naples (Hargrove 111). Regarding tensions between the races in the American military, see Hope.

10. Hargrove (111) suggests another reason for this nickname: black soldiers took hides from the buffalo to protect them from the cold. According to this reading, the insignia suggests the respect that the Indian opponents had for their black conquerors. See Field and Bielakowski for the history of the Buffalo Soldiers. For a personal account of this experience, see the interview on National Public Radio with veteran Joseph Stephenson, who was part of the 92nd Infantry Division during World War II ("Veteran Buffalo Soldier Tells of Service").

11. The original treatment, written by Alfred Hays, ended in the death of the American GI who had promised to take Pasquale home to America: "Dying the black man smiles, and tells him not to make too much of it. He is a poor negro, in America he counts for nothing, he's like a shoeshiner. He's better off not going with him to America. It wouldn't amount to much going there with a poor negro. He's better off staying in Naples. . . ." (qtd. in Wagstaff, *Italian Neorealist Cinema* 243).

12. See Ruberto for a discussion of the cinematic treatment of this phenomenon.

Chapter VI

1. In "The Long March," Brunetta contextualizes the return of American studios to Italy in the postwar period.

2. Woody Allen's *Small Town Crooks* (2000) also revisits this plot.

3. This critique continues in Nanni Moretti's *Caro diario/Dear Diary* (1993) when the director, playing himself, explains to a stranger that he is different from directors who dislike their characters. By way of illustration, he describes the protagonists' actions on the island in Wertmüller's *Swept Away* without naming that film.

4. Michalczyk (250) notes that some critics may have missed the point by interpreting Wertmüller's "fable" literally. He believes that the director wishes to comment on political rather than gender issues on the island.

5. Eleftheriotis (141) examines the American reception of Wertmüller's films and, in his reading, the lack of cultural, political, and historical sensitivity that these reviews demonstrate. He points out that the "impurity" of her films "was a cause for considerable anxiety for the American film

critics, whose demand for political and aesthetic clarity led to either vitri-
olic attacks or theoretically and politically naïve attempts to offer politically
meaningful, definitive readings of her films."

6. The nightclub scenes are well lit, as is the garage in which the
church scene featuring Sammy Davis, Jr. takes place.

7. For a historical discussion of the musical, see Dunne. Altman's
anthology offers a variety of theoretical approaches to the genre.

8. *South Side Story,* inspired by its American filmic namesake *West Side
Story,* which is a retelling of Shakespeare's tale of Romeo and Juliet, recounts
the contested love affair between Romea, a beautiful Nigerian princess, now
a prostitute in Palermo and Giulietto, a street singer. Both "families"—
Giulietto's aunts and Romea's fellow prostitutes—object to the union. This
film directly recalls the *sceneggiata* tradition in the figure of Re Vulcano,
who is played by the most famous contemporary star of that genre, Mario
Merola (1934–2006). As O'Healy (47) notes, this later musical was not so
successful in that neither the Nigerian prostitutes, who were recruited from
the streets to enact their lives, nor audiences embraced it.

9. Muscio (305–324) details the careers of Italian singers such as
Nino Martini who made American films from the advent of sound in the
1930s onwards. Handyside views American musical productions in Europe,
and in France in particular, as a colonizing force. She cites films such as *An
American in Paris* (Minnelli, 1951), *Gentlemen Prefer Blondes* (Hawks, 1953),
and *Funny Face* (Donen, 1957). Although many of the songs were cut when
Stephen Sondheim's Broadway musical *A Funny Thing Happened on the Way
to the Forum* was adapted for the screen in 1966 (directed by Lester, starring
Zero Mostel from the original play), some music remains in this farce.

10. Moretti addresses not only the musical in *Caro diario/Dear Diary,*
a film that I read as the director's philological musings on filmmaking.
Throughout the film, he cites or alludes to films and directors who have
come before him (Pasolini, Wertmüller, Rossellini, Fellini, and others) in an
attempt to understand his place in Italian cinema. This becomes particularly
evident in the second of three "chapters" of the film diary, titled "Islands."
See Marcus (*After Fellini* 285–299) for a reading of Moretti's diseased body
as representative of Italy in this film.

11. See Gallagher ("Land of God" 308–339) about the scandal surrounding the love affair between Rossellini and Bergman. The two versions
of the film, in English and in Italian, emphasize the difference in sensibilities: the American *Stromboli* was twenty-four minutes shorter and much less
ambiguous in its conclusion, whereas the longer Italian version ended with
Karin crying helplessly for God's aid after attempting to flee her stultifying
marriage to Stromboli native Antonio (Mario Vitale), whom she met in a
camp for displaced persons following the war (see Camper).

Chapter VII

1. See Evry for a historical overview of black cowboys in film.

2. *Washington Post* film critic Ann Hornaday, who notes a similarity between Corbijn's aesthetic and that of Antonioni, believes that the Dutch director does not quite live up to Leone's legend. After describing his homage to the master of the spaghetti Western, she argues: "The reference is logical but unearned. What Leone understood, and Corbijn is still learning, is how to deploy the hoariest archetypes in ways that make even pulp entertainment artful and art entertaining."

Bibliography

Abel, Richard. "American Variety and/or Foreign Features: The Throes of Film Distribution." *Americanizing the Movies and "Movie-Mad" Audiences: 1910–1914*. Berkeley: U of California P, 2006. 13–39. Print.

Altman, Rick, ed. *Genre: The Musical: A Reader*. London: Routledge & Kegan Paul, 1981. Print.

Amata, Carmie. "Travolta and DePalma Discuss *Blow Out*." *Brian DePalma Interviews*. Ed. Laurence F. Knapp. Jackson: UP of Mississippi, 2003. 75–81. Print.

Anelli, Maria Teresa, et al. *Fotoromanzo, fascino e pregiudizio: storia, documenti e immagini di un grande fenomeno popolare, 1946–1978*. Milan: Savelli, 1979. Print.

Antonioni, Michelangelo. *The Architecture of Vision*. Ed. Carlo di Carlo and Giorgio Tinazzi. American ed. Marga Cottino-Jones. New York: Marsilio Publishers, 1996. Print.

Antonioni, Michelangelo. *Blow-Up* (Italian screenplay). Torino: Einaudi, 1968. Print.

Arrowsmith, William. *Antonioni: The Poet of Images*. Intro and notes Ted Perry. Oxford: Oxford UP, 1995. Print.

Atkinson, Michael. "About the Production." *The American Official Website*. Focus Features, n.d. Web. 20 June 2011.

Atkinson, Rick. *The Day of Battle: The War in Sicily and Italy, 1943-1944*. New York: Macmillan, 2008. Print.

Banfield, Edward C. *The Moral Basis of a Backward Society*. New York, NY: Free Press, 1958. Print.

Barlow, Aaron. *Quentin Tarantino: Life at the Extremes*. Santa Barbara, CA: Praeger, 2010. Print.

Bazin, André. *What Is Cinema?* Vol. II. Ed. and trans. Hugh Gray. Berkeley: U of California P, 1971. Print.

Beck, Jay. "Citing the Sound: *The Conversation*, *Blow Out* and the Mythological Ontology of the Soundtrack in '70s Film." *Journal of Popular Film & Television* 29.4 (Winter 2002): 156–163. Print.

Bennett, Bruce. "Wrangling Spaghetti Westerns on the Archival Plains." *Wall Street Journal* 29 May 2012. n.pag. Web. 1 June 2012.

Berardinelli, James. "*The American.*" *Reelviews Movie Reviews.* N.p. 1 September 2010. Web. 31 July 2012.

Bertellini, Giorgio. *Italy in Early American Cinema: Race, Landscape, and the Picturesque.* Bloomington, IN: Indiana UP, 2009. Print.

Bigsby, Christopher. *Neil LaBute: Stage and Cinema.* Cambridge: Cambridge UP, 2008. Print.

Bimberg, Edward. *The Moroccan Goums: Tribal Warriors in a Modern War.* Westport, CT: Greenwood Publishing Group, 1999. Print.

Bittini, Patrizia. "Film is Stranger than Fiction: From Cortázar's 'Las babas del diablo' to Antonioni's *Blow-Up.*" *RLA* 7 (1995): 199–203. Print.

Bizio, Silvia. "La carica dei 101 e passa—Storia degli italiani agli Oscar." *Gli italiani di Hollywood: il cinema italiano agli Academy Awards.* Ed. Silvia Bizio and Claudia Laffranchi. Rome: Gremese Editore, 2002. 9–24. Print.

Bliss, Michael. *Brian DePalma.* Metuchen, NJ: The Scarecrow Press, 1983. Print.

Bondanella, Peter. *Hollywood Italians: Dagos, Palookas, Romeo, Wise Guys and Sopranos.* New York: Continuum, 2004. Print.

Bondanella, Peter. *Italian Cinema.* New York: Continuum, 2001. Print.

Bravo, Anna. *Il fotoromanzo.* Bologna: il Mulino, 2003. Print.

Brown, Jeffrey. "Gender, Sexuality, and Toughness: The Bad Girls of Action and Comic Books." *Action Chicks: New Images of Tough Women in Popular Culture.* Ed. Sherrie Inness. New York: Palgrave Macmillan, 2004. 47–74. ebrary Reader. Web. 20 August 2013.

Brunetta, Gian Piero. *Cent'anni di cinema italiano. 1. Dalle origini alla seconda guerra mondiale.* Rome: Editori Laterza, 1995. Print.

Brunetta, Gian Piero. *The History of Italian Cinema: A Guide to Italian Film from Its Origins to the Twenty-First Century.* Trans. Jeremy Parzen. Princeton: Princeton UP, 2003. Print.

Brunetta, Gian Piero. "The Long March of American Cinema in Italy from Fascism to the Cold War." *Hollywood in Europe: Experiences of a Cultural Hegemony.* Ed. David Ellwood and Rob Kroes. Amsterdam: VU UP, 1994. 139–145. Print.

Brunetta, Gian Pietro. *Storia del cinema italiano dal 1945 agli anni ottanta.* Rome: Editori Riuniti, 1982. Print.

Bruno, Giuliana. "The Architecture of Public Melodrama: The Corporeality of the Street." *Streetwalking on a Ruined Map: Cultural Theory and the Films of Elvira Notari.* Princeton: Princeton UP, 1993. 161–183. Google Books. Web. 25 Jan. 2013.

Burr, Ty. "Spike Lee Puts up a Fight; After Knocking the Industry for For-getting Black Troops the Director Offers His Own Take on WWII." *Boston Globe* 21 Sept. 2008. n.pag. Web. 11 Mar. 2010.

Cameron, Ian, and Robin Wood. *Antonioni.* Rev. ed. New York: Praeger, 1971. Print.

Campbell, Duncan. "Saint Quentin." *Guardian* 2 Oct. 2003. n.pag. Web. 6 May 2012.

Camper, Fred. "Volcano Girl." *Chicago Reader* 28 Sept. 2000. n.pag. Web. 15 Jan. 2013.

Canby, Vincent. "Film: Malle's 'Crackers' with Donald Sutherland." *New York Times* 17 Feb. 1984. n.pag. Web. 3 Mar. 2012.

Canby, Vincent. "Screen: A Blow-Up of 'Sweet Charity.'" *New York Times* 2 Apr. 1969. n.pag. Web. 10 June 2012.

Caranti, Chiara. "*Cabiria* 1914 & 1931: la distribuzione in Italia e nel mondo." *Cabiria & Cabiria.* Milan: il castoro, 2006. 148–173. Print.

Cardullo, Bert, ed. *After Neorealism: Italian Filmmakers and Their Films; Essays and Interviews.* Newcastle upon Tyne, UK: Cambridge Scholars Publishing, 2009. Print.

Cardullo, Bert. *De Sica.* Jefferson, NC: McFarland & Company, 2002. Print.

Carolan, Mary Ann McDonald. "Antonioni's Doubting Thomas: Resurrec-tion and Self-Discovery in *Blow-Up*." *Romance Languages Annual* 12 (2003): 203–208. Web. 20 Aug. 2012.

Carolan, Mary Ann McDonald. "Leone's Lone Lady: A New Perspective of Women in *C'era una volta il West*." *Romance Languages Annual* 11 (1999): 261–268. Print.

Casadio, Gianfranco, E.G. Laura, and F. Cristiano, eds. *Telefoni bianchi: Realtà e finzione nella società e nel cinema italiano degli anni quaranta.* Ravenna: Longo Editore, 1991. Print.

Casella, Paola. *Hollywood Italian: gli italiani nell'America di celluloide.* Milan: Baldini & Castoldi, 1998. Print.

Casetti, Francesco, and Luciana Bolme. "Antonioni & Hitchcock: Two Strate-gies of Narrative Investment." *SubStance* 15.3, issue 51: Recent Film Theory in Europe (1986): 69–86. Print.

Cavallero, Jonathan J. *Hollywood's Italian American Filmmakers: Capra, Scorsese, Savoca, Coppola and Tarantino.* Champaign: Illinois UP, 2011. Print.

Cawelti, John G. "Savagery, Civilization and the Western Hero." *Focus on the Western.* Ed. Jack Nachbar. Englewood Cliffs, NJ: Prentice-Hall, 1974. 113–117. Print.

Cawelti, John G. *The Six-Gun Mystique.* 2nd ed. Bowling Green: Bowling Green State UP, 1984. Print.

Christopher, James. "Is Quentin Tarantino Losing the Plots?" *Times (UK)*. 13 Sept. 2007. n.pag. Web. 1 June 2012.

Clair, Jean. "The Road to Damascus." *Focus on Blow-Up*. Ed. Roy Huss. Englewood Cliffs, NJ: Prentice-Hall, 1971. 53–57. Print.

Conard, Mark T. "*Kill Bill:* Tarantino's Oedipal Play." *Quentin Tarantino and Philosophy: How to Philosophize with a Pair of Pliers and a Blowtorch*. Ed. Richard Greene and K. Silem Mohammad. Chicago: Open Court, 2007. 163–175. Print.

Cooke, Paul, ed. *World Cinema's 'Dialogues' with Hollywood*. Basingstoke: Palgrave Macmillan, 2007. Print.

Crowther, Bosley. "The Screen: "Cabiria; Giulietta Masina Stars in Italian Import." *New York Times* 29 Oct. 1957. n.pag. Web. 27 July 2011.

Cuccu, Lorenzo. *Antonioni: il discorso dello sguardo. Da Blow-Up a Identificazione di una donna*. Pisa: ETS Editrice, 1990. Print.

Cumbow, Robert C. *Once upon a Time: The Films of Sergio Leone*. Metuchen, NJ: Scarecrow Press, 1987. Print.

Curle, Howard, and Stephen Snyder. *Vittorio De Sica: Contemporary Perspectives*. Toronto: U of Toronto P, 2000. Print.

D'Agostini, Paolo. "Nine." *La Repubblica. Trova Cinema*. n.d. Web. 22 Feb. 2011.

DeGrazia, Victoria. "Mass Culture and Sovereignty: The American Challenge to European Cinemas, 1920–1960." *Journal of Modern History* 61.1 (Mar. 1989): 53–87. Print.

Del Buono, Oreste. Introduction. "Un esordio difficile." *Lo sceicco bianco*. Milan: Garzanti, 1980. 6–7. Print.

Delisle, Jean, and Judith Woodsworth, eds. *Translators through History*. Amsterdam: John Benjamins Publishing Co., 1995. Print.

De Sica, Vittorio. "De Sica on De Sica." *Vittorio De Sica: Contemporary Perspectives*. Ed. Howard Curle and Stephen Snyder. Toronto: U of Toronto P, 2000. 22–49. Print.

Di Biagi, Flaminio. *Italoamericani tra Hollywood e Cinecittà*. Genova: Le Mani, 2010. Print.

Dodes, Rachel. "After 'Midnight': Woody's Next Act." *Wall Street Journal* 15 June 2012, D4. Print.

Donadio, Rachel. "Getting to 'Nine' by the Italian Route." *New York Times* 11 Dec. 2009. Print.

Drew, William M. *D.W. Griffith's Intolerance: Its Genesis and Its Vision*. Jefferson, N.C. & London: McFarland, 2001. Print.

Dunne, Michael. *American Film Musical Themes and Forms*. Jefferson, NC: McFarland & Company, 2004. Print.

Ebert, Roger. "Interviews: For Gabourey Sidibe, 'Precious' is a Fantasy Come to Life." *RogerEbert.com*. N.p. 26 Oct. 2009. Web. 15 Mar. 2011.

Ebert, Roger. "Kill Bill, Volume 2." *RogerEbert.com.* N.p. 16 Apr. 2004. Web. 10 May 2010.

Ebert, Roger. "The Purple Rose of Cairo." *RogerEbert.com.* N.p. 1 Mar. 1985. Web. 7 July 2010.

Ebert, Roger. "Welcome to Collinwood." *RogerEbert.com.* N.p. 18 Oct. 2002. Web. 23 July 2011.

Eberwein, Robert T. "The Master Text of *Blow-Up.*" *Close Viewings: An Anthology of New Film Criticism.* Ed. Peter Lehman. Tallahassee: Florida State UP, 1992. 262–281. Print.

Eleftheriotis, Dimitris. "Issues of Authorship and the Case of Lina Wertmuller." *Popular Cinemas of Europe: Studies of Texts, Contexts and Frameworks.* New York: Continuum, 2001. 134–152. Print.

Elkin, Frederick. "The Psychological Appeal for Children of the Hollywood B Western." *Focus on the Western.* Ed. Jack Nachbar. Englewood Cliffs, NJ: Prentice-Hall, 1974. 73–77. Print.

Ellenberger, Allan R. *The Valentino Mystique: The Death and Afterlife of the Silent Film Idol.* Jefferson, NC: McFarland & Company, 2005. Print.

Ellwood, David, and Rob Kroes, eds. *Hollywood in Europe: Experiences of a Cultural Hegemony.* Amsterdam: VU UP, 1994. Print.

Elsaesser, Thomas. *European Cinema: Face to Face with Hollywood.* Amsterdam: Amsterdam UP, 2005. Print.

Evry, Max. "African-American Cowboys in Film: A Groundbreaking History of Black Westerns." *Moviefone.* N.p. 18 Dec. 2012 Web. 19 Feb. 2013.

Faustini, Giuseppe. "*La Ciociara* di Moravia: romanzo e film." *La Ciociaria tra letteratura e cinema.* Ed. F. Zangrilli and G. Bonaviri. Pesaro: Metauro Edizioni, 2002. 279–290. Print.

Fellini, Federico. *Fellini on Fellini.* Trans. Isabel Quigley. New York: Da Capo Press, 1996. Print.

Fellini, Federico. *Lo sceicco bianco: con una nota introduttiva di Oreste del Buono e una intervista di Lietta Tornabuoni ad Alberto Sordi.* Milan: Garzanti, 1980. Print.

Fernández, Henry. "From Cortázar to Antonioni: Study of an Adaptation." *Focus on Blow-Up.* Ed. Roy Huss. Englewood Cliffs, NJ: Prentice-Hall, 1971. 163–167. Print.

Ferrini, Franco, ed. *L'antiwestern e il caso Leone.* Rome: Studi Monografici di Bianco e Nero, Centro Sperimentale di Cinematografia, 1971. Print.

Feuer, Jane. *The Hollywood Musical: The Aesthetics of Spectator Involvement in an Entertainment Form.* Bloomington: Indiana UP, 1978. Print.

Feuer, Jane. "The Self-reflective Musical and the Myth of Entertainment." *Genre: The Musical: A Reader.* Ed. Rick Altman. London: Routledge & Kegan Paul, 1981. 159–174. Print.

Field, Ron, and Alexander Bielakowski. *Buffalo Soldiers: African American Troops in the U.S. Forces 1866–1945*. Oxford: Osprey Publishing Ltd., 2008. Print.

Fischer, Austin. *Radical Frontiers in the Spaghetti Western: Politics, Violence and Popular Italian Cinema*. London: I.B. Tauris & Co. Ltd, 2011. ebrary Reader. Web. 20 Nov. 2012.

Forgacs, David, and Stephen Gundle. *Mass Culture and Italian Society from Fascism to the Cold War*. Bloomington: Indiana UP, 2007. ebrary Reader. Web. 6 June 2011.

Foundas, Scott. "Fellini Fantasy Meets Harsh Reality in Rob Marshall's *Nine*." *Village Voice* 15 Dec. 2009. n.pag. Web. 20 Feb. 2013.

Foundas, Scott. "The Next Act." *Directors Guild of America Quarterly*. N.p. Summer 2011. Web. 20 Feb. 2013.

Frayling, Christopher. *Spaghetti Westerns: Cowboys and Europeans from Karl May to Sergio Leone*. London: Routledge & Kegan Paul, 1981. Print.

Freccero, John. "*Blow-Up*: From the Word to the Image." *Focus on Blow-Up*. Ed. Roy Huss. Englewood Cliffs, NJ: Prentice-Hall, 1971. 116–128. Print.

Freeman, Morgan. "A Conversation with Morgan Freeman." Yale University. Woolsey Hall, New Haven, CT. 4 Nov. 2011. Chubb Fellow.

French, Philip. *Westerns: Aspects of a Movie Genre*. London: Secker & Warburg, 1977. Print.

Gallagher, Tag. *The Adventures of Roberto Rossellini: His Life and Films*. Cambridge, MA: Da Capo Press, 1998. Print.

Gardner, Jane F. *Women in Roman Law and Society*. Bloomington: Indiana UP, 1995. Print.

George, Nelson. "Still Too Good, Too Bad or Invisible." *New York Times* 15 Feb. 2013: AR1. Print.

"Gigolo." *Online Etymology Dictionary*. N.p. Web. 13 July 2010.

Giovacchini, Saverio, and Robert Sklar, eds. *Global Neorealism: The Transnational History of a Film Style*. Jackson, MS: Mississippi UP, 2011. ebrary Reader. Web. 13 July 2012.

Gleiberman, Owen. "Cannes: 'The Paperboy,' starring Zac Efron and Nicole Kidman, Proves that 'Precious' Director Lee Daniels Needs Some Common Sense to Go with His Talent." *Inside Movies*. Entertainment Weekly, 24 May 2012. Web. 22 Jan. 2013.

Gonzalez, Ed. "Precious: Based on the Novel by Sapphire." *Slant Magazine* 1 Oct. 2009. Web. 11 Mar. 2010.

Grano, Enzo. *La sceneggiata*. Naples: Attività Bibliografica Editoriale, 1976.

Greene, Richard, and K. Silem Mohammed, eds. *Quentin Tarantino and Philosophy: How to Philosophize with a Pair of Pliers and a Blowtorch*. Chicago: Open Court, 2007. Print.

Guttsman, Janet. "Spike Lee Offers Blood, Hope in World War Two Film." *Reuters*. N.p. 7 Sept. 2008. Web. 11 Mar. 2010.

Hamill, Peter. "Leone: 'I'm a Hunter by Nature, Not a Prey." *American Film* (June 1984): 23–25. Print.

Hamill, Peter. "Once Upon a Time in America." *American Film* (June 1984): 20–25. Print.

Hampton, Benjamin B. *History of the American Film Industry from Its Beginnings to 1931.* New York: Dover Publications, 1970. Print.

Handyside, Fiona. "Colonising the European Utopia." *World Cinema's "Dialogues" with Hollywood.* Ed. P. Cooke. Basingstoke: Palgrave Macmillan, 2007. 138–153. Print.

Hargrove, Hondon B. *Buffalo Soldiers in Italy: Black Americans in World War II.* Jefferson, NC: McFarland & Company, 2003. Print.

Harrison, Carey. "*Blow-Up.*" *Focus on Blow-Up.* Ed. Roy Huss. Englewood Cliffs, NJ: Prentice-Hall, 1971. 39–45. Print.

Haskell, Molly. "Swept Away on a Wave of Sexism." *Village Voice* 29 September 1975. Print.

Hays, Alfred. "Author's Note on the Birth of 'Paisan.'" *New York Times* 7 Mar. 1948 n.pag. Web. 21 February 2013.

Hernandez, Erika. "Kill Bill, Vol. 1 and the Tarantino Game." *AboutFilm.com.* N.p. Nov. 2003. Web. 20 July 2011.

Higson, Andrew, and Richard Maltby, eds. *'Film Europe' And 'Film America': Cinema, Commerce and Cultural Exchange 1920–1939.* Exeter, UK: Exeter UP, 1999. Print.

Hill, Sarah. "Sergio Leone and the Myth of the American West: Once Upon a Time in the West." *Romance Languages Annual* IX (1998): 202–210. Print.

Hirschberg, Lynn. "The Audacity of 'Precious.'" *New York Times* 21 Oct. 2009. n.pag. Web. 20 Jan. 2013.

Hoberman, J. "When Westerns Were Un-American." *New York Review of Books Blog.* N.p. 1 June 2012. Web. 18 July 2012.

Holden, Stephen. "De Niro Packs His Suitcase, Heading to Geezer Territory." *New York Times* 3 Dec. 2009. n.pag. Web. 30 July 2012.

"Hollywood on the Tiber." *Time* 16 Aug. 1954. Print.

Hope, Richard O. *Racial Strife in the U.S. Military.* New York: Praeger Publishers, 1979. Print.

Hornaday, Ann. "George Clooney Isn't Bulletproof." *Washington Post* 1 Sept. 2010. n.pag. Web. 7 Aug. 2012.

Horwitz, Rita, Harriet Harrison, and Wendy White, eds. *George Kleine Collection of Early Motion Pictures in the Library of Congress: A Catalog.* Washington, DC: U.S. Government Print Office, 1980. Print.

Huss, Roy, ed. *Focus on Blow-Up.* Englewood Cliffs, NJ: Prentice-Hall, 1971. 1–6. Print.

"Io, Lo sceicco bianco; Intervista di Lietta Tornabuoni ad Alberto Sordi." *Lo sceicco bianco.* Milan: Garzanti, 1989. 7–20. Print.

Itzkoff, Dave. "That's Amore: Italy as Muse for Woody Allen." *New York Times* 17 June 2012: AR15. Print.

Jameson, Frederic. "Ideology, Narrative Analysis, and Popular Culture." *Theory and Society* 4.4 (1977): 543–559. Print.

Jarratt, Vernon. *The Italian Cinema*. London: Falcon Press, 1951. Print.

Johnson, Charles W. "Epistemology in *Blow-Up*." *Philosophy in Literature*. Vol. II. San Francisco: EMTexts, 1992. 427–515. Print.

Kael, Pauline. "*Blow-Up*: Tourist in the City of Youth." *For Keeps: 30 Years at the Movies*. New York: Penguin, 1994. 900–904. Print.

Kael, Pauline. "Portrait of the Artist as a Young Gadgeteer." *New Yorker* 21 Feb. 2000: 257. Reprinted from 27 July 1981. Print.

Kael, Pauline. "*Shoeshine*." *Vittorio De Sica: Contemporary Perspectives*. Ed. Howard Curle and Stephen Snyder. Toronto: U of Toronto P, 2000. 126–128. Print.

Kakutani, Michiko. "He's a Vessel Overflowing with Rage (and He's the Orphan Son of Precious)." *New York Times* 5 Jul. 2011. C4. Print.

Keel, A. Chester. "The Fiasco of 'Ben Hur': The Hitherto Untold Story of What Happened in Italy and the Supplanting of Ramon Novarro, of George Walsh." *Photoplay* November 1924: 32–33; 101. Print.

Kehr, Dave. "DVDs: Postal Sleuths, Freudian Roiling and Female Revenge." *New York Times* 25 July 2010. 10–11. Print.

Kinder, Marsha. "Antonioni in Transit." *Focus on Blow-Up*. Ed. Roy Huss. Englewood Cliffs, NJ: Prentice-Hall, 1971. 78–88. Print.

Kitses, Jim. "The Western: Ideology and Archetype." *Focus on the Western*. Ed. Jack Nachbar. Englewood Cliffs, NJ: Prentice-Hall, 1974. 64–72. Print.

Knapp, Laurence F., ed. *Brian DePalma Interviews*. Jackson: UP of Mississippi, 2003. Print.

Kramer, Gary M. "Precious & Queer." *Chelsea Now* 11 Dec. 2009. n.pag. Web. 11 Mar. 2010.

Lahr, John. "A Touch of Bad: Why Is the Director Neil LaBute So Interested in Jerks?" *Neil LaBute: A Casebook*. Ed. Gerald C. Wood. New York: Routledge, 2006. 11–22. Print.

Lamar, Howard. *The New Encyclopedia of the American West*. New Haven: Yale UP, 1998. Print.

Landy, Marcia. *Italian Film*. Cambridge: Cambridge UP, 2000. Print.

Lawrence, Will. "Spike Lee gets ready to do battle with Miracle at St Anna," *Telegraph* 2 May 2008. n.pag. Web. 10 Mar. 2010.

Lawson, Carol. "Fellini's 8½ Inspires a Musical." *New York Times* 9 May 1982. n.pag. Web. 15 Feb. 2011.

Leider, Emily. *Dark Lover: The Life and Death of Rudolph Valentino*. New York: Farrar, Straus & Giroux, 2003. Print.

LeRoy, Mervyn. *Mervyn Le Roy: Take One* (as told to Dick Kleiner). New York: Hawthorn Books, 1974. Print.

Liehm, Mira. *Passion and Defiance. Film in Italy from 1942 to Present.* Berkeley: UC Berkeley Press, 1984. Print.

MacKinnon, Kenneth. *Misogyny in the Movies.* Cranbury, NJ: American UP, 1990. Print.

Marcus, Millicent. *After Fellini: National Cinema in the Postmodern Age.* Baltimore: Johns Hopkins UP, 2002. Print.

Marcus, Millicent. *Filmmaking by the Book: Italian Cinema and Adaption.* Baltimore: Johns Hopkins UP, 1992. Print.

Marcus, Millicent. *Italian Film in the Light of Neorealism.* Princeton: Princeton UP, 1987. Print.

Mazzotta, Giuseppe. "The Language of Movies and Antonioni's Double Vision." *Diacritics* 15.2 (1985): 2–10. Print.

McGee, Patrick. *From 'Shane' to 'Kill Bill': Rethinking the Western.* Malden, MA: Blackwell Publishing, 2007. Print.

McGrath, Charles. "Quentin's World: From 'Reservoir Dogs' to "Django Unchained,' How Tarantino Concocted a Genre of His Own." *New York Times* 23 Dec. 2012. AR1; 18–20. Print.

Meeker, Hubert. "*Blow-Up.*" *Focus on Blow-Up.* Ed. Roy Huss. Englewood Cliffs, NJ: Prentice-Hall, 1971. 46–52. Print.

Menarini, Roy. "Kill Bill Vol. 1 & 2." *Quentin Tarantino.* Ed. Vito Zagarrio. Venice: Marsilio, 2009. 91–110. Print.

Miccichè, Lino. *Il cinema italiano degli anni 60.* Venice: Marsilio Editori, 1979. Print.

Michalczyk, John J. *The Italian Political Filmmakers.* Madison, NJ: Fairleigh Dickinson UP, 1986. Print.

Miller, Toby et al. *Global Hollywood.* Berkeley: California UP, 2002. Print.

"Miracle at St. Anna: Spike Lee and James McBride, in a Conversation with Paul Holdengräber." *LIVE from the NYPL.* New York Public Library, 26 Sept. 2008. Web. 10 Sept. 2011.

Modleski, Tania. "Wertmüller's Women *Swept Away* by the Usual Destiny." *Jump Cut* June 1976 (10–11): 1,16. Web. 12 Aug. 2011.

Moravia, Alberto. *La Ciociara* in *Opere complete.* Rome: Bompiani, 1954. Print.

Mulvey, Laura. "Visual Pleasure and Narrative Cinema." *Screen* 16.3 (1975): 6–18. Print.

Mumford, Laura Stempel. *Love and Ideology in the Afternoon: Soap Opera, Women and Television Genre (Arts and Politics of the Everyday).* Bloomington: Indiana UP, 1995. Print.

Murray, Rebecca. " 'Kill Bill Vol. 1' Premiere: Uma Thurman & David Carradine Interviews: 'The Bride' and 'Bill' Discuss Their Roles." *About. com.* n.d. Web. 21 Oct. 2012.

Muscio, Giuliana. *Piccole Italie, grandi schermi: scambi cinematografici tra Italia e Stati Uniti, 1895–1945.* Rome: Bulzoni Editore, 2004. Print.

"Mussolini's Roach." *Time* 4 Oct. 1937. n.pag. Web. 9 Mar. 2009.

Nachbar, Jack, ed. *Focus on the Western.* Englewood Cliffs, NJ: Prentice-Hall, 1974. Print.

Negri, Ada. "Cinematografo." *F/L-Film e Letterature.* Alma Press. n.pag. Web. 19 Aug. 2006.

Negri, Ada. "The Movies." *Unspeakable Women: Selected Stories by Italian Women during Fascism.* Trans. Robin Pickering-Iazzi. New York: The Feminist Press, CUNY, 1993. 58–62. Print.

Nochimson, Martha P. "The Cinecittà Pentimento Effect: A Firsthand Account." *Cineaste* XXXV.2 (2010). n.pag. Web. 12 Oct. 2012.

Nowell-Smith, Geoffrey and Steven Ricci, eds. *Hollywood and Europe: Economics, Culture, National Identity 1945–95.* London: British Film Institute, 1998. Print.

Nuzzi, Paolo, and Ottavio Iemma, eds. *De Sica & Zavattini: parliamo tanto di noi.* Rome: Editori Riuniti, 1997. Print.

O'Healy, Aine. "Reimaging the Voyage to Italy." *Transcultural Feminism in Film and Media (Comparative Feminist Studies).* Ed. Katarzyna Marciniak, Anikó Imre, and Aine O'Healy. New York: Palgrave Macmillan, 2011. 37–52. Ebooks Corporation. Web. 30 July 2012.

Page, Edwin. *Quintessential Tarantino.* London: Marion Boyars Publishers Ltd., 2005. Print.

Pally, Marcia. *"Double* Trouble." *Brian DePalma Interviews.* Ed. Laurence F. Knapp. Jackson: UP Mississippi, 2003. 92–107. Print.

Peary, Gerald. "Interviews: Neil LaBute." *GeraldPeary.com.* Oct. 2000. Web. 19 July 2010.

Peary, Gerald. *Quentin Tarantino: Interviews.* Jackson: UP of Mississippi, 1998. Print.

Pezzotta, Alberto. *Il western italiano.* Milan: il castoro, 2012. Print.

Pisa, Nick. "Spike Lee's Miracle at St Anna Denounced by Italian War Veterans as 'Insulting.'" *Telegraph* 30 Sept. 2008. n.pag. Web. 6 May 2012.

Pontuale, Francesco. *In Their Own Terms: American Literary Historiography in the United States and Italy.* New York: Peter Lang, 2007. Print.

Prats, A. J. *The Autonomous Image: Cinematic Narration and Humanism.* Lexington: UP of Kentucky, 1981. Print.

Pratt, Annis. *Archetypal Patterns in Women's Fiction.* Bloomington: Indiana UP, 1982. Print.

Pullella, Philip. "Woody Allen's 'To Rome, With Love' Opens in Eternal City." *Thomson Reuters* 13 Apr. 2012. n.pag. Web. 15 June 2012.

"Quo vadis? at Astor: Moving Pictures of Famous Story of Rome Shown for First Time Here." *New York Times* 22 Apr. 1913. n.pag. Web. 20 Apr. 2010.

Ricci, Steven. *Cinema and Fascism: Italian Film and Society 1922–1945.* Berkeley: U of California P, 2008. Print.

Richards, John C. and James Flamberg. *Nurse Betty: The Shooting Script (Newmarket Shooting Script).* New York: Newmarket Press, 2000. Print.

Rifkin, Ned. *Antonioni's Visual Language.* Ann Arbor, MI: U of Michigan Research P, 1982. Print.

Risset, Jacqueline. "*The White Sheik*: The Annunciation Made to Federico.' *Perspectives on Federico Fellini.* Ed. Peter Bondanella and Cristina Degli-Esposti. New York: G.K. Hall & Co., 1993. 63–69. Print.

Robson, Leo. "Tarantino Unchained." *Financial Times* 12 Jan. 2013, Life & Arts: 1–2. Print.

Rosenbaum, Jonathan. "The White Sheik." *Current.* The Criterion Collection, 28 Apr. 2003. Web. 24 July 2012.

Ruberto, Laura. "Neorealism and Contemporary European Immigration." *Italian NeoRealism and Global Cinema.* Ed. Laura E. Ruberto and Kristi M. Wilson. Detroit: Wayne State UP, 2007. 242–258. Print.

Ruberto, Laura E., and Kristi M. Wilson, eds. *Italian NeoRealism and Global Cinema.* Detroit: Wayne State UP, 2007. Print.

Rushing, Robert A. "The Real of Desire Travel/Detection/Hitchcock/Antonioni." *The Communication Review* 6.4 (2003): 313–326. Print.

Samuels, Charles Thomas. *Encountering Directors.* New York: G.P. Putnam's Sons, 1972. Print.

Sapphire. *Push: A Novel.* New York: Vintage Contemporaries/Vintage Books, 1997. Print.

Sapphire. *The Kid: A Novel.* New York. Penguin, 2011. Print.

Sarris, Andrew. "No Antoniennui." *Focus on Blow-Up.* Ed. Roy Huss. Englewood Cliffs, NJ: Prentice-Hall, 1971. 31–35. Print.

Scorsese, Martin. "Un'incredibile bellezza." *Cabiria & Cabiria.* Torino: il castro, 2006. 9. Print.

Sciolino, Elaine. "Camera in Hand, Italian at Heart: The Cinematography of Darius Khondji." *New York Times* 15 July 2012. n.pag. Web. 25 July 2012.

Scott, A. O. "The Black, the White and the Angry." *New York Times* 24 Dec. 2012. C1. Print.

Scott, A. O. "Miracle at St. Anna (2008): Hollywood War, Revised Edition." *New York Times* 25 Sept. 2008. n.pag. Web. 19 Nov. 2011.

Scott, A. O. " 'Nine': There Will Be Lingerie (Singing, Too)." *New York Times* 17 Dec. 2009. n.pag. Web. 10 Jan. 2010.

Scott, A. O. "'Precious': Howls of a Life, Buried Deep Within." *New York Times* 5 Nov. 2009. n.pag. Web. 15 Jan. 2013.

Scott, A. O. "Topsy-Turvy." *New York Times Magazine* 9 Dec. 2012: 42–46. Print.

Scott, A. O., and Manohla Dargis. "When Do We 'Get It'? This Season's Challenging Films Guide Viewers Beyond Simple Storytelling." *New York Times* 25 Nov. 2012: AR1, AR14. Print.

Segrave, Kerry. *American Films Abroad: Hollywood's Domination of the World's Movie Screens from the 1890s to the Present.* Jefferson, NC: McFarland & Company, 1997. Print.

Simsolo, Noël. *Conversations avec Sergio Leone.* Paris: Stock, 1987. Print.

Smith, Harry T. "The Italian Film in America." *Italica* 15.2 (1938): 63–65. Print.

Soares, Andre. *Beyond Paradise: The Life of Ramon Novarro.* New York: St. Martin's Press, 2002. Print.

Sorlin, Pierre. *Italian National Cinema: 1896–1996.* London: Routledge, 2001.

Steimatsky, N. "The Cinecittà Refugee Camp (1944–50)." *MIT Press Journal* (Oct. 2009): 23–50. Print.

Stevens, Dana. "The Really Quiet American: George Clooney in a Contemplative Spy Thriller." *Slate* 1 Sept. 2010. n.pag. Web. 10 Dec. 2010.

Tamburri, Anthony Julian. *Re-viewing Italian Americana: Generalities and Specificities on Cinema.* New York: Bordighera Press, 2011. Print.

Tarantino, Quentin. "Quentin Tarantino Tackles Old Dixie by Way of the Old West (by Way of Italy)." *New York Times Magazine* 27 Sep. 2012: MM45. Print.

Teloitte, J. P. "Interrogating the Real in Neil LaBute's Films." *Neil LaBute: A Casebook.* Ed. Gerald C. Wood. New York: Routledge, 2006. 125–139. Print.

"That's Amore: Italy as Muse for Woody Allen." *New York Times* 17 June 2012: 9. Print.

The American Official Site. Focus Features. n.d. Web. 1 May 2011.

The George Kleine Collection of Early Motion Pictures in the Library of Congress: A Catalog. Ed. Rita Horwitz and Harriet Harrison. Washington, DC: Library of Congress, 1980. Print.

"The Personal Puff." *Time* 2 Aug. 1926. n.pag. Web. 17 Mar. 2009.

Thompson, Kristin. *Exporting Entertainment: America in the World Film Market, 1907–34.* London: British Film Institute, 1985. Print.

Tomasulo, Frank P. "'You're Tellin' Me You Didn't See': Hitchcock's *Rear Window* and Antonioni's *Blow-Up*." *After Hitchcock: Influence, Imitation & Intertextuality.* Ed. David Boyd and R. Barton Palmer. Austin: University of Texas Press, 2006. 145–172. Print.

Tornabuoni, Lietta. "Nine." *L'Espresso. Trova Cinema.* n.d. Web. 22 Feb. 2011.

Toro, Gabe. "Woody Allen Talks the Inspiration of Italian Cinema for 'To Rome with Love.'" *The Playlist.* Indiewire, 21 June 2012. Web. 24 July 2012.

Treveri Gennari, Daniela. *Post-War Italian Cinema: American Intervention, Vatican Interests.* New York: Routledge, 2009. Print.

Vallely, Jean. "Brian DePalma: The New Hitchcock or Just Another Rip-Off?" *Brian DePalma Interviews.* Ed. Laurence F. Knapp. Jackson: UP of Mississippi, 2003. 69–74. Print.

Van Watson, William. "Luchino Visconti's (Homosexual) *Ossessione.*" *Reviewing Fascism: Italian Cinema, 1922–1943.* Ed. Jacqueline Reich and Piero Garofalo. Bloomington: Indiana UP, 2002. 172–193. Print.

Verrill, Addison. "Sweet Charity." *BoxOffice* 3 Feb. 1969: 10. Print.

"Veteran Buffalo Soldier Tells of Service." *National Public Radio.* 11 Nov. 2008. Web. 7 Jan. 2013.

Vitti, Antonio. "La Ciociaria nel cinema." *La Ciociaria tra letteratura e cinema.* Ed. Zangrilli Franco. Pesaro: Metauro Edizioni, 2002. 291–305. Print.

Vivarelli, Nick. "Cinecittà Staffers Call Off Strike." *Variety* 30 Sept. 2012. n.pag. Web. 10 Nov. 2012.

Wagstaff, Christopher. "A Forkful of Westerns: Industry, Audiences and the Italian Western." *Popular European Cinema.* Ed. Richard Dyer and Ginette Vincendeau. Abingdon, UK and New York: Routledge, 1992. 245–262. Print.

Wagstaff, Christopher. *Italian Neorealist Cinema: An Aesthetic Approach.* Toronto: U of Toronto P, 2007. Print.

Ward, Richard Lewis. *A History of the Hal Roach Studios.* Carbondale: Southern Illinois University, 2006. Print.

Warshow, Robert. "Movie Chronicle: The Westerner." *Focus on the Western.* Ed. Jack Nachbar. Englewood Cliffs, NJ: Prentice-Hall, 1974. 45–56. Print.

Wright, Will. *Sixguns & Society. A Structural Study of the Western.* Berkeley: U of California P, 1975. Print.

Wyke, Maria. *Projecting the Past: Ancient Rome, Cinema and History.* London: Routledge, 1997. Print.

Zagarrio, Vito. *Quentin Tarantino.* Venice: Marsilia, 2009. Print.

Zavattini, Cesare. "Some Ideas on the Cinema." *Vittorio De Sica: Contemporary Perspectives.* Ed. Howard Curle and Stephen Snyder. Toronto: U of Toronto P, 2000. 50–61. Print.

Zeffirelli, Franco. *Autobiografia.* Milan: Mondadori, 2006. Print.

Zonta, Dario. "Nine é il musical tradito ispirato all'inimitabile '8 ½' e ricco di star, il film non ha ironia né magia." *L'Unità* 22 Jan. 2010. n.pag. Web. 12 Apr. 2012.

Filmography

Blow Out. Screenplay by Brian De Palma. Dir. Brian De Palma. Perf. John Travolta and Nancy Allen. 1981. The Criterion Collection, 2011. DVD.

Blow-Up. Screenplay by Michelangelo Antonioni and Tonino Guerra. Dir. Michelangelo Antonioni. Perf. Vanessa Redgrave and David Hemmings. 1966. MGM, 2004. DVD.

Kill Bill, Vol. 1. Screenplay by Quentin Tarantino. Dir. Quentin Tarantino. Perf. Uma Thurman and Daryl Hannah. 2003. Miramax Films, 2004. DVD

Kill Bill, Vol. 2. Screenplay by Quentin Tarantino. Dir. Quentin Tarantino. Perf. Uma Thurman and David Carradine. 2004. Miramax, 2004. DVD.

Miracle at St. Anna. Screenplay by James McBride. Dir. Spike Lee. Perf. Derek Luke and Michael Ealy. 2008. Touchstone Home Entertainment, 2009. DVD.

Nurse Betty. Screenplay by James Flamberg and John C. Richards. Dir. Neil LaBute. Perf. Renée Zellweger and Morgan Freeman. 2000. Polygram USA Video, 2001. DVD.

Once Upon a Time in the West. Screenplay by Sergio Leone, Bernardo Bertolucci, Dario Argento, Mickey Knox and Sergio Donati. Dir. Sergio Leone. Perf. Claudia Cardinale, Henry Fonda, and Charles Bronson. 1968. Paramount Pictures, 2003. DVD.

Precious: Based on the Novel "Push" by Sapphire. Screenplay by Jeffrey S. Fletcher. Dir. Lee Daniels. Perf. Gabourey Sidibe and Mo'Nique. 2009. Lionsgate, 2010. DVD.

The Purple Rose of Cairo. Screenplay by Woody Allen. Dir. Woody Allen. Perf. Mia Farrow and Jeff Daniels. 1985. MGM, 2001. DVD.

The White Sheik. Screenplay by Federico Fellini, Michelangelo Antonioni, Tullio Pinelli, and Ennio Flaiano. Dir. Federico Fellini. Perf. Alberto Sordi, Brunella Bovo and Leopoldo Trieste. 1952. The Criterion Collection, 2003. DVD.

Two Women. Screenplay by Vittorio De Sica and Cesare Zavattini. Dir. Vittorio De Sica. Perf. Sophia Loren, Eleonora Brown, and Jean-Paul Belmondo. 1960. Alpha Video, 2004. DVD.

Index

Note: Page numbers in *italics* indicate illustrations.

Accorsi, Stefano, 116
Agustin, Julio, 120
Aiello, Danny, 26
Albanese, Antonio, 17, 109
Alfieri Law, 27, 89
Allen, Nancy, 47
Allen, Woody, 3; on escapist movies, 32; on Italian movies, 15, 16; *Annie Hall*, 15; *Celebrity*, 16; *Purple Rose of Cairo*, 13, 16, 20, 26–33, *28*, *29*, *31*, 40–43, 126; *Small Town Crooks*, 146n2; *Stardust Memories*, 15, 122; *To Rome with Love*, 13, 15–18
Alonso, Laz, 104
Ambrosio film company, 5, 6
The American, 135–38
Anderson, Paul Thomas, 134
Anderson, Wes, 13
Anthony, Eugene, 28
Antonioni, Michelangelo, 3, 145n4; *Blow-Up*, 13, 15, 45–59, *48*, *52*, 133; *L'amorosa menzogna/Lies of Love*, 17; *Red Desert*, 17
Applegate, Christina, 120
Arthur, Jean, 72
Astaire, Fred, 31, 32, 126
Atkinson, Michael, 137–38

Baker, Josephine, 103
Baldwin, James, 103
Banfield, Edward, 144n7
Baraldi, Angela, 46
Baranski, Christine, 110
Barlow, Aaron, 80, 82
Barrymore, Drew, 116
Barrymore, Lionel, 8
Bazin, André: on neorealism, 91, 93, 94; on Westerns, 61, 67–69
Beals, Jennifer, 128
Beckinsale, Kate, 116, *118*
Belafonte, Harry, 132
Ben-Hur (Niblo), 8–10, *9*
Ben-Hur (Wyler), 12
Benigni, Roberto, 16–17
Berardinelli, James, 138
Bergman, Ingmar: *Face to Face*, 15
Bergman, Ingrid, 129, 147n11
Bertellini, Giorgio, 2, 139n4
Bicycle Thieves/Ladri di biciclette, 15, *86*, 91, 94, 95, 97, 103, 106
Bigelow, Kathryn, 113
Bigsby, Christopher, 36
bildungsroman, 41
Bilson, Rachel, 116
Biograph film company, 7
Bizio, Silvia, 3

Bliss, Michael, 57, 142n10
Blow-Up, 13, 15, 45–59, *48*, *52*,
133
Boetticher, Budd, 72, 75
The Bold and the Beautiful (TV
series), 128–29
Bondanella, Peter, 2
Booth, Martin, 137
Borgnine, Ernest, 76
Bovo, Brunella, 18, *21*
Bowles, Peter, 51
Boyden, Peter, 47
Brabin, Charles, 9, 10
Brando, Marlon, 46
Brest, Martin: *Scent of a Woman*,
110–12, *111*
Bronson, Charles, 64, *65*, 66, *67*,
72
Brooks, Mel: *Blazing Saddles*, 132
Brooks, Richard: *The Professionals*,
72
Brown, Eleonora, 95, *99*
Brown, Jeffrey, 80
Brunetta, Gian Piero, 7–8, 63,
86–87
Budd, Billy, 103
Buffalo Soldiers, 104, *105*, 146n10
Burr, Ty, 105
Burton, Richard, 12

Cabiria (Pastrone), 4–6, 120
Cain, James M., 89
Calamai, Clara, 90
Calvino, Italo, 140
Cameron, James: *The Terminator*,
80
Campion, Jane, 113
Canby, Vincent, 110, 121–22
Capitani, Giorgio, 63
Caranti, Chiara, 4, 139n2
Cardinale, Claudia, 64, *70*, 72–73
Cardullo, Bert, 145n6

Carey, Anne, 137
Carey, Mariah, 92, 97
Carito, Gaetano, 116
Caro diario/Dear Diary, *127*,
127–29, 146n3
Carpentieri, Renato, 128
Carradine, David, 64
Casadio, Gianfranco, 27, 140n8
Casella, Paola, 2–3
Casetti, Francesco, 49
Castellari, Enzo, 74
Castle, John, 48
Cavalli, Valeria, *117*
Cawelti, John G., 62, 63, 143n1
Centro Sperimentale di Cinemato-
grafia, 11
Chase, David: *Not Fade Away*, 46
Chenal, Pierre: *Le dernier tournant*,
89
Cinecittà, 1–2, 4; Mussolini and,
10–11; privatization of, 12–13
Cines film studio, 5, 6, 9
Clooney, George, 110, 135–38
Coen brothers, 36
Coleman, Cy, 120, 122
Colman, Ronald, 8
commedia all'italiana, 41
Conard, Mark T., 77, 81
The Conversation, 46, 50
Cooper, Gary, 74
Coppola, Francis Ford, 1, 50; *The
Conversation*, 46, 50; *The Godfa-
ther*, 13
Coppola, Sofia, 113
Corbijn, Anton: *The American*,
135–38
Corbucci, Sergio, 13–14, 63, 76;
Django, 74, 144n9
Cortázar, Julio, 56, 142n9
Cosby, Bill, 132
Craig, Daniel, 62
Crist, Judith, 141n2

Crowther, Bosley, 118, 121
Cruz, Penélope, 18, 124
Cuccu, Lorenzo, 141n1
Culp, Robert, 76
Cumbow, Robert C., 69, 71, 72, 73

D'Agostini, Paolo, 124–25
Damiani, Damiano, 63
Daniels, Jeff, 26, *28*, 30, *31*
Daniels, Lee, 3, 85, 88, 102, 107;
    Monster's Ball, 96; *Paperboy*, 91;
    Precious, 14, 90–102, *98*, *100*
Dante Alighieri, 78
Dargis, Manohla, 134
Dassin, Jules: *Rififi*, 110
Davis, Miles, 103
Day-Lewis, Daniel, *123*, 124
De Niro, Robert, 116, 117, *118*
De Palma, Brian, 3, 141n4; on
    Coppola, 50; on Hitchcock,
    49–50; *Blow Out*, 13, 15, 45–59,
    54, 133; *Greetings*, 49; *Hi, Mom!*,
    49
De Sica, Vittorio, 3, 88, 93; *La
    Ciociara/Two Women*, 95–102,
    99, *100*; *Ladri di biciclette/Bicycle
    Thieves*, 15, *86*, 91, 94, 95, 97,
    106; *Miracle in Milan*, 145n6;
    Sciuscià/Shoeshine, 15, 91, 97;
    Umberto D., 91, 97
Dear Diary/Caro diario, *127*,
    127–29, 146n3
Delisle, Jean, 88
Delli Colli, Tonino, 65
DeMille, Cecil B., 4
Demme, Jonathan: *Married to the
    Mob*, 42
Dench, Judi, 124
Depp, Johnny, 62
Di Biagi, Flaminio, 2
DiCaprio, Leonardo, 74, 76

Dickinson, Angie, 72
Dietrich, Marlene, 72
DiMauro, Claudio, 116
Divorce Italian Style, 41
Django (Corbucci), 74, 144n9
Django Unchained (Tarantino), 74,
    76, 131–33
Dreyfus, Julie, 78

Eastwood, Clint, 62, 136; *Unfor-
    given*, 132
Ebert, Roger, 30, 92, 110
Eberwein, Robert T., 142n12
Eckhart, Aaron, 35
Edison, Thomas, 3, 7
Edwards, Gavin, 74
8½, 14, 16, *122*, 122–25
Eisenberg, Jesse, 17
Ekberg, Anita, 16–17
Elam, Jack, 66–67, 76
Eleftheriotis, Dimitris, 114, 146n5
Elsaesser, Thomas, 134–35, 138
Ente Nazionale Importazione Pel-
    licole Estere (ENAIPE), 139n6
Ente nazionale industrie cinemato-
    grafiche (ENIC), 11
Everybody's Fine, 14, 116–17, *118*

Fairbanks, Douglas, 20
Farrow, Mia, 26, *28*, *29*, 30, *31*
Faustini, Giuseppe, 96
Favreau, Jon: *Cowboys and Aliens*,
    62
Fellini, Federico, 3; on film end-
    ings, 32; influence on Woody
    Allen of, 15, 16; remakes of,
    117–18; *Amarcord*, 15; *I Clowns*,
    17; *8½*, 14, 16, *122*, 122–25;
    Ginger and Fred, 28, 141n9;
    Intervista/Interview, 28; *La dolce
    vita*, 12, 16–17, 28; *Luci del
    varietà/Variety Lights*, 27–28;

Fellini, Federico *(continued)*
*Notti di Cabiria/Nights of
Cabiria*, 13, 16–18, 117–21,
119; *Lo sceicco bianco/The White
Sheik*, 13, 16–29, *21*, *24*, 33,
40–43
Ferrell, Will, 61
Ferrini, Franco, 68
Ferzetti, Gabriele, 64
Feuer, Jane, 126
Fields, Dorothy, 120, 122
Film Forum (2012), 63
Fischer, Austin, 131–32
Fitzmaurice, George: *The Eternal
City* (film), 8; *The Son of the
Sheik*, 18
Flamberg, James, 36
Flashdance, 128
Fonda, Henry, 64, 66, *67*, 72, 135,
136
Ford, Harrison, 62
Ford, John: *Sargeant Rutledge*, 132
Fosse, Bob: *Sweet Charity*, 118–21,
119, 125, 126
fotoromanzi (photo magazines), 13,
21–25, *24*, 28, 39, 140n5. *See
also* soap operas
Foundas, Scott, 85, 124
Fox, Vivica, 78
Foxx, Jamie, 74
Franz, Dennis, 47
Frayling, Christopher, 62, 71, 73,
144n7
Freeman, Morgan, 35, 36, 132,
141n10
French, Philip, 68, 69, 143n6
Freud, Sigmund, 110

Gallagher, Tag, 106, 147n11
Gangs of New York (Scorsese), 1, 13
García Márquez, Gabriel, 4

Garnett, Tay: *The Postman Always
Rings Twice*, 89
Gassman, Vittorio, 110–12
General Film Company, 6, 7
Germi, Pietro: *Divorzio all'italiana/
Divorce Italian Style*, 41; *The
Road to Hope*, 145n6; *Sedotta ed
abbandonata/Seduced and Aban-
doned*, 41
Giannini, Adriano, 115–16
Giannini, Giancarlo, 112, *113*
Ginger and Fred, 28, 141n9
Giovacchini, Saverio, 90
Girotti, Massimo, 90
Gish, Lillian, 8
Gleiberman, Owen, 91
Goldman, Bo, 111, 112
Goldstein, Bruce, 63
Goldwyn, Tony: *The Last Kiss*, 14,
116
González, Edlyn, 120
Gordon, Nealla, 97
Griffith, D. W., 4–5; *Intolerance*, 5;
Judith of Bethulia, 5
Grindhouse, 132, 144n10
Groundhog Day (Ramis), 109
Guazzoni, Enrico: *Quo vadis?*, 5–7,
7, 46, 109

Haggis, Paul: *Third Person*, 13
Hamill, Peter, 143n4, 143n5
Hamilton, Linda, 80
Handyside, Fiona, 147n9
Hannah, Daryl, 78
Hargrove, Hondon B., 104, 146n9,
146n10
Harrison, Carey, 142n12
Haskell, Molly, 113–14
Hawn, Goldie, 114, *115*
Hays, Alfred, 106, 146n11
Helmond, Katherine, 114

Hemingway, Anthony: *Red Tails*, 102

Hemingway, Ernest, 88

Hemmings, David, 45, *48, 52*

Hermann, Edward, 114

Heston, Charlton, 12

Hill, Sarah, 144n8

Hilton, Nicky, 12

Hirschberg, Lynn, 92, 93, 94

Hitchcock, Alfred, 49–50; *Psycho*, 47

Holden, Stephen, 117

Holdengräber, Paul, 103

Hornaday, Ann, 148n2

Hudson, Kate, *123*, 124

Hull, Edith Maude, 20

Inglorious Bastards (Castellari), 74

Inglourious Basterds (Tarantino), 74, 82

Itala-film company, 5–6

Italian film industry, 27; early years of, 4–7; after World War I, 8, 9; after World War II, 11–12, 109–10

Italian New Left movement, 132

Itzkoff, Dave, 15

Janney, Allison, 39

Jarratt, Vernon, 5, 139n6

Jeffries, Herb, 132

Joffe, Rowan, 137

Johnson, Hylan "Dots," 106

Jones, Kirk: *Everybody's Fine*, 14, 116–17, *118*

Kael, Pauline, 57–58, 141n2

Kakutani, Michiko, 94

Kalem Company, 6–7

Kennedy, Burt: *Hannie Caulder*, 75–76

Kennedy, Edward M., 50

Kennedy, John F., 50

Keyes, Ken, Jr., 93

Khondji, Darius, 140n1

Kidman, Nicole, 124

Kill Bill, 14, 63, 64, 75–83, *79*, 132

Kim, Helen, 81

King, Henry, 8

Kinnear, Greg, 33, *35*

Kleine, George, 6–7, 109, 139n4

Kopechne, Mary Jo, 50

Kopit, Arthur, 122

Kristeva, Julia, 110

La Ciociara/Two Women, 95–102, *99, 100*

La dolce vita, 12, 16–17, 28

LaBute, Neil, 3; *In the Company of Men*, 36; *Nurse Betty*, 13, 16, 20, 33–43, *34, 35*

Lacan, Jacques, 110

Ladri di biciclette/Bicycle Thieves, 15, *86*, 91, 94, 95, 97, 106

Laffranchi, Claudia, 3

Lahr, John, 37

LaMarr, Barbara, 8

Landa, Juan de, 90

Landy, Marcia, 145n7

The Last Kiss, 14, 116

Lattuada, Alberto, 28

Lawson, Carol, 123–24

Lee, Ang: *Crouching Tiger, Hidden Dragon*, 80

Lee, Spike, 3, 88, 132 33; *Miracle at St. Anna*, 14, 90–91, 102–7, *105*, 132

Leider, Emily, 10, 140n3

Leone, Sergio, 3, 13–14, 148n2; legacy of, 74, 138; pseudonym of, 143n5; *A Fistful of Dollars*,

Leone, Sergio *(continued)*
    62; *C'era una volta il West/Once
    Upon a Time in the West*, 14,
    62–73, *65*, *67*, *70*, 77–83, 131,
    135–36, *136*; *Duck, You Sucker*,
    144n13; *For a Few Dollars More*,
    62; *The Good, the Bad and the
    Ugly*, 62
Leone, Vincenzo, 143n5
LeRoy, Mervyn: *Quo vadis?*, 11–12,
    46, 109
Lester, Richard: *A Funny Thing
    Happened on the Way to the
    Forum*, 147n9
The Life Aquatic with Steve Zissou,
    13
Lindstrom, Petter, 129
Lithgow, John, 47
Little, Cleavon, 132
Liu, Chia Hui, 76
Liu, Lucy, 78
Lizzani, Carlo, 63
Long, Samuel, 6
The Longest Day, 104
Loren, Sophia, 124; in *Two Women*,
    95, 96, 98, *99*, 145n4; in *Quo
    vadis?*, 12
Lucas, George, 102
Lucas, Henry Lee, 128
Lumière brothers, 3
L'unione cinematografica educativa
    (LUCE), 11
Lyne, Adrian: *Flashdance*, 128

Machiavelli, Niccolò, 83
MacKinnon, Kenneth, 49–50
MacLaine, Shirley, *119*, 120–22
Macy, William, 110
Madsen, Michael, 78
Maggiorani, Lamberto, *86*, 106
Magnani, Anna, *87*
Malle, Louis: *Crackers*, 110

Manfredonia, Giulio: *È già ieri/
    Stork Day*, 109
Mangini, Maria Luisa, 120
Mankiewicz, Joseph L.: *Cleopatra*,
    12
Mann, Anthony, 74
Marcus, Millicent, 85, 95, 97, 101,
    113, 127, 145n4
Marion, Frank J., 6
Marshall, Garry: *Overboard*,
    114–15, *115*
Marshall, Rob: *Nine*, 14, 122–23,
    123
Martin, Strother, 76
Martini, Nino, 147n9
Mascetti, Gina, 22
Masina, Giulietta, 18, 118–22, *119*
Mastroianni, Marcello, 16; in *8½*,
    124; in *Ginger & Fred*, 141n9;
    in *I soliti ignoti*, 110; in *Stanno
    tutti bene*, 116, *117*
Mastronardi, Alessandra, 17
Matrix, 80
May, Curt, 51
Mayer, Louis B., 9, 10
Mazzotta, Giuseppe, 142n11
McBride, James, 103–5
McDowall, Roddy, 114
McGee, Patrick, 75
McNaughton, John: *Henry: Portrait
    of a Serial Killer*, 128
Melato, Mariangelo, 112, *113*
Melford, George: *The Sheik*, 18,
    19, 20
Memento, 134
Menarini, Roy, 75
Merola, Mario, 147n8
Mezzogiorno, Giovanna, 116
Miccichè, Lino, 62, 63, 143n3
Michalczyk, John J., 146n4
Miles, Sarah, 48
Miller, Omar Benson, 106

"mind-game films," 134–35
Miracle at St. Anna, 14, 90–91, 102–7, *105*, 132
Modleski, Tania, 113–14
Momo, Alessandro, 111
Monicelli, Mario: *I soliti ignoti/Big Deal on Madonna Street*, 110
Mo'Nique (actor), 92, 93, 98, *98*
Montalban, Ricardo, 121
Morante, Elsa, 95
Moravia, Alberto, 88, 95, 96, 145n4
Moretti, Nanni: *Aprile/April*, 128; *Caro diario/Dear Diary*, *127*, 127–29, 146n3
Morricone, Ennio, 65, 74, 117, 131
Moss, Carrie-Anne, 80
Mostel, Zero, 147n9
Muccino, Gabriele: *L'ultimo bacio/The Last Kiss*, 14, 116
Mulvey, Laura, 48–49, 72, 73
Mumford, Laura Stempel, 38
Murray, Bill, 109
Murray, Rebecca, 76
Muscio, Giuliana, 2, 147n9
Mussolini, Benito, 9–11, 89
Mussolini, Vittorio, 11, 89
Muti, Ornella, 17

Nachbar, Jack, 61
Nazzari, Amedeo, 120
Negri, Ada, 24–26
Nelson, Christopher Allen, 77
neorealism, 85–88, *86*, *87*, 90, 94, 97, 103, 104
Nero, Franco, 74
Newell, Mike: *Love in the Time of Cholera*, 4
Newfield: *Harlem on the Prairie*, 132
Niblo, Fred: *Ben-Hur*, 8–10, *9*

Nights of Cabiria, 18, 117–21, *119*
Nine, 14, 122–23, *123*
Nochimson, Martha P., 13
Nolan, Christopher, 134
Not Fade Away, 46
Novarro, Ramon, 9
Nurse Betty, 13, 16, 20, 33–43, *34*, *35*

O'Donnell, Chris, 111, *111*
O'Hara, Maureen, 72
O'Healy, Aine, 126–27, 147n8
Once Upon a Time in the West, 14, 62–73, *65*, *67*, *70*, 77–83, 131, 135–36, *136*
opera, 11, 17
organized crime, 127, 144n7
Ovid, 101

Pacino, Al, *111*, 111–12
Page, Edwin, 75, 76
Paisan, 103, 105–6
Pally, Marcia, 141n4
paparazzi, 16
Parolini, Gianfranco, 63
Pasca, Alfonsino, 106
Pastrone, Giovanni: *Cabiria*, 4–6, 120
Patton, Paula, 97
Pavese, Cesare, 88
Peary, Gerald, 36
Peckinpah, Sam, 74
"pentimento effect," 13
Perry, Tyler, 93
Pezzotta, Alberto, 144n9
Pfeiffer, Michelle, 42
Piccioni, Piero, 112
Piedmont, Matt: *Casa de mi padre*, 61
Poitier, Sidney: *Buck and the Preacher*, 132
Ponti, Carlo, 17, 145n4

The Postman Always Rings Twice, 89
Powell, Quisha, 97, *98*
Pratt, Annis, 40, 41
Procacci, Domenico, 116
Propp, Vladimir, 82
Pulp Fiction, 76, 131
Purple Rose of Cairo, 13, 16, 20, 26–33, *28*, *29*, *31*, 40–43, 126

Quel maladetto treno blindato/Inglorious Bastards (Castellari), 74
Quo vadis, baby?, 46
Quo vadis? (Guazzoni), 5–7, *7*, 46, 109
Quo vadis? (LeRoy), 11–12, 46, 109

Rafelson, Bob, *89*
Ramis, Harold: *Groundhog Day*, 109
Rawhide (TV series), 62, 136
Redgrave, Vanessa, 47
Reservoir Dogs, 76
Richards, John C., 36
Ridley, Alice Tan, 92
Rifkin, Ned, 142n12
Risi, Dino, 96; *Profumo di Donna*, 110–12
Risset, Jacqueline, 21
Ritchie, Guy, 112, 114; *Swept Away*, 115–16
Roach, Hal, 11, 89
Roach, Jay: *The Spy Who Shagged Me*, 46
Robards, Jason, 64
Rock, Chris, 35
Rockwell, Alexandre, 128
Rockwell, Sam, 110
Rodriguez, Robert: *Grindhouse*, 132, 144n10
Rogers, Ginger, 31, 126
Romola, 8

Rossellini, Roberto, 16, 102, 103; *Paisà/Paisan*, 105–6; *Roma città aperta/Rome Open City*, 86, 86–88, 91, 106; *Stromboli, terra di Dio*, 129, 147n11
Rota, Nino, 125
Ruberto, Laura E., 90
Russell, Kurt, 114, *115*
Russo, Anthony & Joe, 110

Salvatores, Gabriele: *Quo vadis, baby?*, 46
Sandrelli, Stefania, 116
Sandrich, Mark: *Top Hat*, 31, 126
Santesso, Walter, 16
Sapphire (author), 93, 94
sceneggiata (Neapolitan musical), 127
Scent of a Woman, 110–12, *111*
Sciabordi, Matteo, 103
Scorsese, Martin: *Gangs of New York*, 1, 13; *My Voyage to Italy*, 4
Scott, A. O., 83, 124, 132, 134
Scott, Ridley: *Alien*, 80
Seven Beauties, 113
Shakespeare, William, 101, 147n8
The Sheik, 18, *19*, 20
Shoeshine, 15, 91, 97
Sidibe, Gabourey, 92, *92*, 93, *98*
Sienkiewicz, Henryk, 6
Simon, Neil: *Sweet Charity*, 117–18, *119*, 120, 122
Simsolo, Noël, 69
Sklar, Robert, 90
slavery, 132–33
soap operas, 128–29; Mumford on, 38; in *Nurse Betty*, 33–34, 37–38, 40, 42. See also *fotoromanzi*
Solinas, Franco, 63
Solli, Sergio, 17
Sollima, Sergio, 63

The Son of the Sheik, 18
Sondheim, Stephen, 147n9
Sordi, Alberto, 18, 21, *21*, 23, 140n5
spaghetti Westerns: creation of, 13–14, 62; elements of, 62–68; recent films and, 131–38; Tarantino on, 74–75, 131. *See also* Westerns
Spielberg, Steven: *Lincoln*, 132
The Spy Who Shagged Me, 46
Staiola, Enzo, *86*, 106
Stanno tutti bene, 14, 116–17, *117*
Stardust Memories, 15, 122
Stella, Martina, 116
Stephenson, Joseph, 146n10
Stevens, Dana, 137
Stewart, Jimmy, 74
Stewart, Jon, 102
Strode, Woody, 66–67, 132
Stromboli, terra di Dio, 129, 147n11
Swackhamer, E. W.: *Man and Boy*, 132
Sweet Charity, 118–21, *119*, 125, 126
Swept Away (Ritchie), 115–16
Swept Away (Wertmüller), 112–15, *113*, 133, 146n3

Tamburri, Anthony Julian, 2
Tarantino, Quentin, 3; on spaghetti Westerns, 74–75, 131; *Death Proof*, 144n10; *Django Unchained*, 74, 76, 131–33; *Grindhouse*, 132, 144n10; *Inglourious Basterds*, 74, 82; *Kill Bill*, 14, 63, 64, 75–83, *79*, 132; *Pulp Fiction*, 76, 131; *Reservoir Dogs*, 76
Taviani, Paolo & Vittorio: *Good Morning, Babylon*, 139n3

Taylor, Elizabeth, 12
telefoni bianchi comedies, 27, 86
The Terminator, 80
Thurman, Uma, 64, *79*, 81
To Rome with Love, 13, 15–18
Top Hat, 31, 126
Tornabuoni, Lietta, 125
Tornatore, Giuseppe: *Stanno tutti bene*, 14, 116–17, *117*
Torre, Roberta, 126–27, 147n8
Travolta, John, 46, *54*
Tuskegee Airmen, 102
Two Women/La Ciociara, 95–102, *99*, *100*
Tykwer, Tom: *Cloud Atlas*, 134

L'ultimo bacio/The Last Kiss, 14, 116
Umberto D., 91, 97
uncanniness, 110

Valentino, Rudolph, 9–10, 13, 18–20, 140n3, 140n4; in *The Sheik*, 18, *19*, 20; in *The Son of the Sheik*, 18
Valenza, Tasia, 110
Valerii, Tonino, 63
Vallan, Giulia D'Agnolo, 63
Vallely, Jean, 50
Vallone, Raf, 97
Van Watson, William, 89
Vanzina, Stefano: *La poliziotta/Policewoman*, 112
Variety Lights, 27–28
Venice Film Festival, founding of, 11
Verbinski, Gore: *Rango*, 61–62
Verdon, Gwen, 120
verismo movement, 88
Verrill, Addison, 121
Vietnam War, 63, 143n4
Visconti, Luchino, 87; *Bellissima*, 145n6; *Ossessione/Obsession*, 89–90

Vitale, Mario, 147n11
Vitti, Antonio, 95
Vittorini, Elio, 88

Wachowski, Larry/Lana: *Matrix*, 80
Wagstaff, Christopher, 106
Walsh, George, 9
Waltz, Christoph, 74
Warshow, Robert, 61, 69
Washington, Kerry, 74
Wayne, John, 62, 104
Welch, Raquel, 75–76
Wertmüller, Lina: *Seven Beauties*,
    113; *Swept Away*, 112–15, *113*,
    133, 146n3
Westerns, 61–62, 66–69; Mafia
    families and, 144n7; plot lines
    of, 144n12. *See also* spaghetti
    Westerns

The White Sheik, 13, 16–29, *21*,
    24, 33, 40–43
Wilson, Kristi M., 90, 144n1
Winfrey, Oprah, 93
Wolff, Frank, 64
Woodsworth, Judith, 88
Wright, Will, 77–79, 144n12
Wyler, William: *Ben-Hur*, 12

Yeoh, Michelle, 80
Yeston, Maury, 123–24

Zapruder film, 50
Zavattini, Cesare, 85, 87, 90, 91,
    93
Zeffirelli, Franco, 17, 145n4
Zellweger, Renée, 34, *34*, *35*, *36*
Zola, Émile, 88
Zonta, Dario, 125